Sue Lawley's
DESERT ISLAND DISCUSSIONS

Sue Lawley's
DESERT ISLAND
DISCUSSIONS

Photographs by
Nicholas Read

Hodder & Stoughton
LONDON SYDNEY AUCKLAND TORONTO

Illustrations by Lee Ebbrell

British Library Cataloguing in Publication Data

Lawley, Sue
   Sue Lawley's desert island discussions.
   1. Great Brtain. Radio programmes. Sound disc programmes
   I. Title
   791.4472

   ISBN 0-304-52230-5

Published by Hodder and Stoughton,
a division of Hodder and Stoughton Ltd,
Mill Road, Dunton Green, Sevenoaks, Kent TN13 2YA.
Editorial Office: 47 Bedford Square, London WC1B 3DP.

Photoset by Rowland Phototypesetting Ltd,
Bury St Edmunds, Suffolk

Printed in Great Britain by
Butler and Tanner Ltd,
Frome and London

Contents

Complete list of Sue Lawley's guests on *Desert Island Discs* from March 1988 to December 1989, their eight records, their book and their luxury.

Acknowledgements

I would like to thank Olivia Seligman, the producer of *Desert Island Discs*; Rosemary Edgerley, the programme's researcher; and Stephanie Mewies, its production assistant. Without their dedication and professionalism there would be no programme and therefore no book. I would also like to thank David Harman of the BBC's Gramophone Library, who cast his practised eye over the appendix of my castaways' records, making many corrections and improvements, and Ion Trewin of Hodder and Stoughton who believed in the project from the beginning and has been gently encouraging to the end.

Thanks are due too to Nick Read, our photographer, and his wife Christine, whose organisation of the pictures for this book was a triumph of diplomacy, and to Christine Fisher who typed and retyped my manuscript as well as helping out in many other ways.

Finally I would like to thank my husbund, Hugh, to whom this book is dedicated. I have leaned heavily on his skills as a manager, his perceptions as a critic and, occasionally, his talents as a writer.

Sue Lawley

*In the lists of the castaways' records
at the end of each chapter, their
favourites are printed in bold type.*

INTRODUCTION

Studio B16 is about as far removed from a desert island as you could imagine. No ray of sunshine, or any other form of weather for that matter, penetrates its basement walls. Tucked away at the end of a maze of corridors it is cleaned quite often, but always dusty. It is also the victim of an eccentric central heating system which allows for only two temperatures – stifling heat or freezing cold. As a place to visit, it has nothing to recommend it.

As a place in which to record *Desert Island Discs*, however, it is perfect. Once I find myself sitting across the green baize table from my guest, the producer and studio manager staring at us intently through the window of the cubicle while the tape machine turns slowly alongside them, studio B16's bleakness becomes its greatest asset. Its neutrality is suddenly transformed into a world: the hectic political world of Neil Kinnock or Enoch Powell; the amusing theatrical world of Athene Seyler or Michael Gambon; or the fantastic, farcical world of Dame Edna Everage. Memory, imagination, the power of the human voice – and, of course, eight pieces of music – are all it takes to convert this grey corner of the BBC's Broadcasting House in London into the most popular desert island in the world.

Therein lies the secret of *Desert Island Discs*. The invitation to appear on it is as much an accolade as it was during the forty-four years it was run by its creator, Roy Plomley. For these reasons, once someone has agreed to take part, he or she has to enter fully into the spirit of the programme. Castaways must give of themselves and help create a picture of their world. To that extent it will be recorded very much on their terms. Its success will depend on how much they want to give, how much they dare reveal. I may be asking the questions, and delving quite deeply as I do so, but *Desert Island Discs* is not a programme of penetrating interviews or sensational revelations. It is a conversation built around a selection of musical excerpts and, like all good conversations, it works best as a partnership.

In the autumn of 1987 I heard that Michael Parkinson was leaving the programme. He had taken care of it ever since Roy Plomley's death two years earlier. At that time many people thought *Desert Island Discs* would

1

disappear, but the BBC decided to keep it going with a new presenter. I had been one of Michael's castaways. Could I now change places and become mistress of this precious radio island?

I wanted to very much indeed – however, unlike many other jobs in broadcasting, it wasn't one for which you could apply. Then came the call: was I prepared to have my name put on a shortlist of people whom the BBC was considering for the job? I consented with embarrassing alacrity. Two weeks later I was told it was mine. If I had felt honoured at being chosen as a castaway, I felt ennobled now.

I knew that *Desert Island Discs* was one of the most prestigious programmes on BBC Radio and I was sure that if I handled it well my reputation would not suffer. I was attracted to it for those reasons – but they were not the only ones. My experience in television had taught me that people enjoy listening to good talk. They like to hear about the famous and the distinguished in a way which is simple, pleasing and revealing, without being prying or intrusive. *Desert Island Discs* struck me as the perfect setting for that kind of broadcasting. Because it is such a good programme for its guests, it is a good programme for the interviewer as well. Those reasons were as important to me as any others. By Christmas 1987 it had been announced that I had become the new custodian. I recorded my first programme the following February. It was transmitted at the end of March.

My first three castaways were Lord Hailsham, Jane Asher and Arthur Scargill. I think those three names say a lot about my attitude towards the programme. Lord Hailsham is eminent and distinguished, Jane Asher intelligent, attractive and popular, Arthur Scargill important and controversial. For me, these descriptions span the areas which *Desert Island Discs* can and should cover. It is a programme which may be at the heart of things, or slightly removed, surveying them. It loves the present, but enjoys the past just as much. It is properly impressed by power, wealth and ambition, but it knows that the world is made up of more than that. In other words, it enjoys people. Music alone cannot make the desert island habitable or attractive: it is people's thoughts and observations related to their music which do that.

Each programme is recorded in advance. The producer, Olivia Seligman, and I agree the list of people we'd like to invite. We are always receiving suggestions, from publishers, friends and people we bump into in corridors and at parties, but ours is the final choice. Once someone has agreed to be 'cast away' and a recording date arranged, the programme's researcher, Rosemary Edgerley, goes to visit the person concerned.

Roy Plomley used to give his guests lunch in the Garrick Club and then take them on a leisurely tour of the BBC Gramophone Library before settling down to do a recording. Indeed, in the very early days he was required to script the whole interview. Then he and his guest would read out their 'conversation' for the recording. I dislike talking to an interviewee in advance. I worry that it will spoil the spontaneity of our exchange. So I steer well clear of any meeting until the appointed hour. All of which makes Rosemary's task that much more important. She has to find out what reminiscences have prompted the selection of records, book and luxury. This is a more difficult task than it sounds. Very rarely have people decided all these things. They're generally pleased to have been asked (hardly anyone refuses our invitation) and are looking forward to making their choices. The task of doing it, however, they often find very difficult. It is surprising how many lists of records have been the subject of agonising revision or last-minute change. David Owen arrived at the studio stuck on ten records. Eventually, he managed to drop Herb Alpert and his Tijuana Brass and Dvořák. Lenny Henry vacillated between Vivaldi and Funkadelic and the Archbishop of Canterbury spent at least ten minutes weighing up the relative merits of Harvey and the Wallbangers as against Fats Waller.

Rosemary always comes back with what we need to begin work on the structure and shape of the programme. Olivia disappears with the list of records to the BBC Gramophone Library whose encyclopaedic knowledge of composers, conductors, opus numbers and everything else to do with music is one of our greatest comforts – and I, armed with notes, thoughts, newspaper cuttings and anything else I need, begin work on *my* contribution.

The only way to do an extensive interview with someone is to read about them until you have soaked them up. So if my castaway has written books, I read some of them. I read Douglas Hurd's thrillers, re-read Salman Rushdie's *Midnight's Children*, more Penelope Lively and, of course, many an autobiography. In the case of Bob Hoskins I made sure I had seen his films such as *Mona Lisa* and *The Long Good Friday*. I mention this, not to show how assiduous I am, but to demonstrate how necessary I believe it is to get as close to the person you are interviewing as possible. When you have read about their lives, from cuttings or newspaper interviews, and then read, watched or listened to their work, you spot recurring themes and begin to create a sense of who it is you are about to meet. Once this process is over I sit down at my desk in front of my typewriter and try to feel the person around me. The first thing I write is the introduction. Only when I have finished that do I feel able to embark on the interview itself. Starting is always the most difficult part. After that the structure begins to take shape, the questions begin to flow and the person, I hope, is given space and opportunity to emerge.

Inevitably, the structure of the programme is built around each of the eight pieces of music. Quite often I decide the order in which the music is to be played. I don't override what the castaway wants – that would be wrong — but it's surprising how often people appearing on the programme do not mind about the sequence of their music. The temptation is always to play the pieces in chronological order, beginning with echoes of childhood and ending with something more mature and reflective. But this doesn't always happen and, in any case, could become tedious. I work at the shape of the programme for several hours until at last a final structure has emerged. At this stage I am either very pleased or rather depressed. If I am pleased I know that the person is there, waiting to talk to me. If I am depressed, I know that he or she has in some way eluded me; that the recording is going to be a testing one. Whatever my state of mind, I phone Olivia, the producer. This conversation always takes place the day before the actual recording. We go through everything together — the questions, the music, and any other details that may be necessary. We make changes, dropping questions and adding new ones. We rephrase and argue with ourselves about whether or not certain areas should be included. Eventually we finish. We shall meet next in Studio B16, in the basement of Broadcasting House, where we shall try and summon up another castaway's world.

A sense of occasion is very important to a recording of *Desert Island Discs*. Despite the limitations of the studio, we try to make the process as special as we can. We start with the music, making sure that the guest is happy with the selection. Sometimes we haven't been able to discover the version they have requested — we play the one we have found to make sure they like it. It is important to remember that quite often we can be playing music which someone has not heard for years. And we have to be careful not to play the full extract that we want to use in the final programme. That could spoil the castaway's reaction, which we like to keep as fresh as we can. Occasionally, of course, we are dealing with music that our guests have provided themselves. Neil Kinnock wanted a recording of 'Horace the Horse' sung by his daughter, Rachel; Sir Nicholas Henderson to hear a tape of his grandson playing the violin; Tony Benn a madrigal composed by his son. Such gems as these are beyond the resources of even the most indefatigable BBC librarian. They come with the castaway — and we listen to them for the first time in the cubicle outside the studio. It can also happen that a memory has deceived. I will always remember Athene Seyler, who was coming up to her hundredth birthday at the time, telling us that she wanted a Chopin étude, but could not remember which one. She hummed it, but nobody recognised it. She hummed it again but still the work remained a mystery. We began to play the études to her, but the more she heard the more she shook her head. The piece she wanted could not be found. Finally, two young men from the library made their way to the studio. They sat next to her in reverential silence as once again she hummed her chosen Chopin. Then she stopped: we all waited expectantly. "It's a waltz," said one of the librarians calmly. "The one in C sharp minor actually. I'll go and fetch it now." Athene Seyler beamed happily. At least she had been right about the composer.

Eventually the castaway and I find ourselves sitting opposite each other in the studio ready to begin the main recording for the programme. Each edition of *Desert Island Discs* contains about twenty-eight minutes of talk and twelve minutes of music. We record much more than that. It is quite common for us to put about fifty minutes of conversation on tape.

I began by trying to record, almost to the minute, the length of interview required, rather as one does a live television interview. But I quickly discovered that such an approach destroyed the natural rhythm of the programme. A castaway must never be hurried, or pressed into arriving at the next high point in his or her life, and should only be interrupted for the sake of clarity. This is what gives each programme its individuality and its producer, Olivia, enormous problems.

Often a castaway takes five minutes to tell a story which, however significant, cannot justify a large slice of the programme. Some are wedded to the chronology of their lives or a list of specific names and places which don't always enhance their stories. Sometimes, I'm afraid, they are led by me along less than compelling avenues of their existence. The fact that little of this comes to the notice of the listener is entirely due to Olivia's skill and long hours at the editing machine. I have rarely experienced any disappointment or felt that my producer has 'lost' a treasured interchange. Furthermore, if our castaways have spotted the missing minutes they have, so far at least, been too polite to complain.

We also play more of the music than will eventually be heard on the air. This is an important aspect of the recording. A piece of music combined with a person's thought, observation or memory is a very potent force and one of the keys to the success of *Desert Island Discs* as a radio programme. It is a moment which cannot be skimped or glossed over. As the guest leads me to the chosen piece, I nod, and it begins to play through the speakers, I am always aware that we have reached a very telling moment. As the music starts I watch closely for any reaction on the part of the castaway. Sometimes it is simply relaxation – the lighting of a cigarette, the leaning back in a chair, a moment of rest before the next clutch of reminiscences. Sometimes it is simply a break – an excuse to ask questions or to nip along the corridor to the lavatory. But sometimes it is a moment of great profundity. The conjunction of an important moment in a person's life with a piece of much-loved music can create a situation of enormous intensity. As the music fills the studio it can prompt many different reactions – a warm smile, a look of frowning concentration, or even eyes full of tears. Sir Claus Moser nearly wept when he told the story of how the Royal Opera House mounted a special performance of *The Marriage of Figaro* for him and his wife when he retired as Chairman of the Trustees.

When the cast bowed in his direction at the end of the opera, he felt, he said, as though Mozart might have written it for him.

Rowan Atkinson was deeply moved by memories of his Oxford days with Richard Curtis, still a friend and collaborator. The record he had chosen to remind him of their university days together was 'Still Crazy After All These Years'. When we played it, it made him cry. I always feel that it is at moments like these that *Desert Island Discs* comes into its own. The guest on the programme has led me and the audience quite naturally and openly to a moment of huge importance in his or her life. The programme touches it and then moves on. It does not stop and dwell or linger to poke and pry. It has no need to. The memory and the music have said all that need be said.

Slowly, patiently, the programme unwinds. All of us have become unaware of the unprepossessing surroundings in which we find ourselves. The whole of our concentration goes into the recording. I think the last part is always the easiest. If people are often unsure about their final selection of records, or the order in which they are to be played, they always seem to know how they want to end. Arthur Scargill, I recall, was insistent that whatever else happened, the last piece of music played on his programme was the Hebrew Slaves' Chorus from Verdi's *Nabucco*. After that I ask them which of the eight records they would like above all others. In my experience, the act of listening to them all again has often changed their original decision. Away from a record player or a tape machine they often think that they know which is the most precious to them. But when they have heard them all through and put them in the context of their lives, that decision sometimes changes.

It is surprising how often a simple melody or a popular song cuts through the years to revive a treasured memory. I was interested that a distinguished conductor such as Jeffrey Tate, most of whose records fell into the category of serious music, ended with Billie Holiday singing 'I'll Be Seeing You'. What is more, that was the one he wanted to keep when the waves washed the others away.

The business of choosing records is a curious one. It is a game we all play but when it comes to the moment when you have to declare on BBC Radio your chosen eight – it takes on an almost frightening significance. This is your last choice. It will stay with you for ever. The world will judge you by it. By your eight tunes shall it know you and make final assessments of your tastes and attitudes. I know from my own experience just how worrying this process of selection can be. I can still think about the choices I made for my programme with Michael Parkinson (it included music by the Beatles, Rachmaninov, Purcell and Ella Fitzgerald) and wonder whether I got it right. Would I change it if I were asked again? Probably.

Nevertheless, people do have certain self-imposed guidelines. They often choose records they would like played at their memorial service. Thora Hird picked 'Onward Christian Soldiers' for this reason. Slightly eccentric records often crop up too. They add a little spice and show another side of the person being interviewed. Rabbi Lionel Blue chose a very unusual song by Cicely Courtneidge, 'Why Has the Cow Got Four Legs?' and Sir Stephen Spender included a pre-war music-hall song called 'I'm a Tree' by Douglas Byng. But I suppose the golden rule is to choose the eight records that you feel you would want at the moment of being asked on to the programme. Enjoy it for what it is – a rather serious and, I hope, fulfilling game.

Perhaps as you read this you have begun to make up your own list of records. Don't worry about it. Most people do. If your selection includes a little Wagner you are in very distinguished company: Stephen Spender, Enoch Powell, Gerald Scarfe, Jeffrey Tate, Sir Claus Moser, Stephen Fry, Diana Mosley and Lord Dacre all chose music by him. And if you opted for *Götterdämmerung* I think you will find that many of them did too. Perhaps you are one of those who was affected by the death of John Lennon and want something with which to remember that moment. You are not alone there either, as the choices of Bob Hoskins and Michael Gambon testify. So carry on with your list. Make it as personal as you can. Choose records because they remind you of people, things or times. Or choose them simply because they have stayed with you and enriched your life. Choose popular melodies and great classical works; choose funny little out-of-the-way pieces and recordings of the spoken voice. Choose something only you possess – or choose a tune the whole world knows by heart. In other words, choose what you like. But make sure it belongs to you and is of you.

In this book I have had to make another selection – twenty of the interviews I have done for *Desert Island Discs*. The final list was as difficult to compile as any choice of eight records, but I hope it represents the range and variety of the programme.

At the end of every recording I always ask my interviewee: "Did you enjoy that?" Perhaps this book will help you to share my enjoyment of *Desert Island Discs* and that of the people who have appeared on it with me. It is a unique programme, as popular now as when it was first broadcast in 1942. Its popularity is, I believe, due to the fact that it is a perfect example of the radio art. It marries music with conversation and creates life. The desert island is as crowded or as lonely as the castaway wants it to be. One thing, however, is certain. Whether it is noisy or quiet, reflective or brash, serious or comic, it is a place that the radio audience will always want to share.

ENOCH POWELL

I don't think Enoch Powell was terribly pleased with his interview on *Desert Island Discs*. He had come, he told me later, armed with an instruction from his wife to show the warm side of his character. Anyone who knows him can be in no doubt that it exists. He likes to twinkle, and sometimes refers to himself as an "old cove". I'm afraid, however, that there weren't many twinkly bits in our radio programme together. Instead we heard from the classical scholar, poet and soldier with a passionate sense of nationhood. He chose Wagner, Beethoven and one piece of Haydn as company on his desert island – great, serious works imbued with a strong moral flavour. Never mind: if Mr Powell didn't twinkle, he certainly sparkled – with an intelligence and clarity of mind that made this one of our most successful editions of *Desert Island Discs*.

Enoch Powell has never held any of the great offices of state. But lack of position has never undermined his influence. He remains a fixture in our minds long after those who got better jobs have faded from them. Appetite for debate has killed his hunger for power. That's what makes him such a compelling public figure.

"I assumed I would be killed in the war . . . I suppose
I have been lastingly ashamed of myself that it
wasn't what happened."

Enoch Powell shouldn't really be called 'Enoch' at all. Throughout his childhood his name was John — but he changed it in his teens for what he said was "a very mundane" reason. Mundane isn't quite the word I would use for a young man who so wanted to produce the definitive edition of Thucydides that he was upset when he found a scholar of the same name writing on the same subject.

"It must have been when I was sixteen or seventeen, I came across a copy of the *Classical Review* in which an article on Thucydides had been written by an Oxford scholar by the name of J. U. Powell. "'Heavens,' said I to myself, 'we shall be confused — I must differentiate myself from this fellow, whoever he is, who is writing about Thucydides', so for the first time I spelt Enoch in full and that became my cheque signature and that became my permanent signature."

So we have a classical scholar to thank for giving us one of the more unusual Christian names in post-war politics. How did its owner view the idea of being a castaway?

"I think it's cruel of you to do this. Man is a social animal and to take him and put him, with whatever conveniences and commodities, in isolation is an affront to his humanity. In selecting music for your purposes, I have selected that to which I would look for long-enduring pabulum on which I could feed both my intellect and my emotions."

'Pabulum', for those of us less well versed in the classics than Mr Powell, means 'food for the mind'. And that, in turn, means Wagner because Enoch Powell has been under his influence for as long as he can remember. He wanted to hear something from each of the four parts of *The Ring* because, he said, it is "a whole cycle of thought and of events, a moral cycle and an intellectual cycle, lived through as you witness and hear it". Great stuff — even if it wasn't quite what Mrs Powell had in mind when she briefed him on being warm.

If, by now, you have a picture of the young Powell as a very serious and intelligent child, you would be right. Did he carry off all the school prizes?

"I'm afraid so."

Both his parents were teachers and his mother obviously took great pains with his education. "She was the person who first taught me Greek, for she had taught herself Greek in her youth in Newport, Shropshire, at the college there."

Listening to Enoch Powell's words again and transcribing them for the purpose of this book, I'm struck by how deep that classical education must have gone. The phrasing of his sentences is beautifully correct. So, too, is the whole structure of his speech: very few people these days would use the word 'for' rather than 'because' in conversation.

But was this clever, prize-winning schoolboy popular?

"I wasn't conscious of being unpopular, and certainly I enjoyed the company of my school-fellows."

Did he have a nickname?

"Well, I had a nickname at the secondary school which I attended before I went to King Edward's Grammar School and that was 'scowly-powly' owing to my habit of frowning, which I think I probably still have."

"Why do you think you frowned so much?"

"Everyone has facial habits and characteristics and mine was a contraction or furrowing of the brow – I needn't explain it or apologise for it further."

"I presume it was accepted, without question, that you would go up to Oxford or Cambridge?"

"To go with a scholarship or bursary to Oxford or Cambridge was the natural expectation of those in the upper sixth form at King Edward's, Birmingham."

Cold on the page, that all comes across as a very curt exchange. It wasn't. There is the ghost of a smile behind that rat-a-tat-tat narrative. You can't read it, but you can hear it when it's spoken.

After we had played more Wagner – 'Siegmund's Spring Song' from *Die Walküre* – Mr Powell referred to its climax, where "human affection and human love have a sense of being in tune with nature". Could he remember, I asked him, when he first fell in love?

"Yes . . . yes, I remember that. But I'm not telling."

"You've written about it in your poetry, haven't you?"

"Yes, I've written about it in poetry. I've written about it therefore in the way in which it alone should be written about."

"So there are times when your heart has ruled your head?"

"I'm not sure that my head is ever wholly intellectually controlled. I think the power behind my use of my intellect is of an emotional character, and I think that there's a strong pent-up force of emotion which drives me, even when I appear to be most in search of a logical answer to an intellectual question."

Enoch Powell went to Cambridge, to Trinity College, where, naturally, he achieved a Double First. He thinks now that he was an "absurdly studious" undergraduate. He would get up at five o'clock in the morning to work on his translation of Herodotus and became, in his words, "a learning machine". It was only later, when he became a fellow of Trinity, that he learned to enjoy the society of an institution.

As I listened to him talk and as we played more Wagner – each extract used as a signpost in his life – I became aware that the young Mr Powell must have been extraordinarily intense. Working at a furious pace, with the great themes of the classics and Wagner ringing in his head, he seemed an unlikely person to take up politics as a career. What changed him? Up to the war, he said, music was one of the most important things in his life. As a schoolboy he had thought that he might become a professional musician (presumably when resting from that definitive edition of Thucydides). After the war, however, he had kept away from it. Was that because it moved him too much?

"I suppose I am a bit afraid of it," he said. Suddenly I was in front of a different Enoch Powell. We had found a change, a turning-point in his life. It was the war itself.

"Having anticipated the war, as I did from 1934-5 onwards, and having regarded my existence as only provisional until it came, and having, when it did come, with such joy and relief taken part in it, I emerged, to my surprise, into a full span of human existence. I had not lived before in a world other than a world terminable by catastrophe. And here was a world which went on for ever – a normal world."

"You believed you were going to die in the war?"

"I assumed I would be killed in it. That was a natural assumption. After all, the average expectation of life of an infantry officer in November 1918 was three weeks, and as I was determined to be an infantry officer, I assumed that that was what would happen. And I suppose I've been lastingly ashamed of myself that it wasn't what happened."

"Can you remember the moment when you realised you were not going to die?"

"Yes, it's very vivid. It was a moment in 1944. I was in India and it was the night that a monsoon broke, and I did what everybody else does on the night that the monsoon breaks – I walked out from under the verandah, and stood in the rain and got soaked. And I suddenly said to myself, 'What are you going to do then? – the chances now are that you will survive, so what are you going to do? There will be a life, a world after the war. What are you going to do?' And it happened to me as I think it happens to most people when what externally seems to be a major decision is taken: you don't actually take the decision, the decision was there. It's like hearing a knock on the door – you open the door and there's somebody standing on the doorstep, and what was standing on the doorstep was, 'You will go into politics'."

"Why do you say that you would like to have been killed in the war?"

"I think this is something commonly felt by those who served but from whom life was not demanded in the war."

"But was that not very hurtful to your family?"

"I'm not conscious that my daughters were terribly shocked."

"And your wife?"

"My wife, I think, tended to take it personally. But wives do, don't they?"

"I think I can understand that she would."

"But I'm not thereby seeking to invalidate anything that I've done, or tried to do, or been imagined to do, since 1945. It's simply that a mark is placed upon men, not merely by service in the armed forces, but by emerging from the war. It's a mark which I think they bear for the rest of their days."

I find that a fascinating passage. It seems to me to be an extraordinary mixture of humanity and cruelty, of self-sacrifice and self-indulgence. It makes me think again of the intense young man who had been transformed by war into a successful politician. Perhaps that's why its experience was so important to him. The real Enoch Powell is, above all else, a disciplined and patriotic soldier who, convinced of the rightness of the cause he defends, marches unblinkingly towards the sound of gunfire.

And so we had come to politics at last. First of all I wanted to explore why it was that Enoch Powell, whose intellect and standing commanded so much respect, never achieved the kind of office he might have expected.

"At that level, office is a lottery, and certainly the highest of all offices is more a lottery than the other offices. But at any stage in my career there was a price that I was not prepared to pay for improving my chances in the lottery. I'm not criticising others who regard it as a game which is played for office – I've no objection to people who play a game and play it according to the rules – but my disposition was in the last resort, I suppose, to make my own rules."

Had it been a source of enormous frustration to him?

"You're not talking to a frustrated man. You're talking to a man who admittedly lost his place in the assembly where for thirty-seven years he had been happy and in that sense fulfilled, but you're also talking to a man who, in losing it, has missed his constituency more than he misses the House of Commons, and who is finding, to his astonishment, that his mind remains active, inquisitive, critical, and defiant, as his years decline."

Having established that Mr Powell views his political career with reasonable equanimity, we moved to one of its great central episodes – his 1968 speech on immigration. He was calling, I reminded him, for the immediate reduction in numbers of immigrants coming into Britain and for the repatriation of many of those already here.

"That was the official policy of the Conservative Party at the time," he said.

Then why did Edward Heath sack him for saying it?

"Because he didn't like the fact that it had been heard. It was the *tone*, not the content. He *never* claimed that the contents were incompatible with the policy of the party."

"He said it was racialist in tone."

"He disliked the tone. It's significant that the word 'tone' was used. After all, we're talking about a musician."

That struck me as a rather waspish remark. Why did he suddenly feel the need to sting? I pressed on. It perhaps wasn't surprising, I said, that Mr Heath hadn't liked the tone. Mr Powell had talked about the indigenous population not being able to find hospital beds to give birth to their children. Suddenly, he pounced. "I didn't say that," he retorted. "You're not quoting. You're saying what you think I said."

I am, I'm afraid, too old a hand to go unarmed into interviews with men like Enoch Powell. I had the text of the speech in front of me. My reply was to quote directly:

> They found their wives unable to obtain hospital beds in childbirth, their children unable to obtain school places, their homes and neighbourhoods changed beyond recognition, their plans and prospects for the future defeated.

"I'll stand by all that," he replied. "It was a description of the circumstances in which many hundreds of thousands of people were already living, and many more hundreds of thousands were shortly to find themselves living."

In saying that, I think Mr Powell was accepting that I had quoted him accurately the first time. I still don't know what he planned to say when I tackled him on this point, but he had obviously been surprised by it. Perhaps he thought that the desert island would be no place for such clamorous stuff. But it was – and so it should be.

Having established the exact content of his 'Rivers of Blood' speech, as it became known, I asked him whether he still believed, as he had said twenty years previously, that the growth of immigrant communities could result in tremendous upheaval, even civil war.

"Yes," he answered. "I still regard that as the prospect." Quite obviously Mr Powell had no regrets whatsoever about the words he spoke that day.

He talked next about the second time he deeply shocked his colleagues. This was six years later, in 1974, when he left the Conservative Party on the Common Market issue and advised people to vote Labour.

"They shouldn't have been shocked. They hadn't been listening to me saying for years that there are some issues which override party. One issue which overrides party is the independence of the nation which I believed then, and believe now – though I've been joined by others in the meantime – is endangered, indeed is sacrificed, by Britain being part of the European Economic Community."

14

But why had he gone so far as to encourage the electorate to vote for another party?

"I was no longer a candidate, no longer a member of the Conservative Party, which I ceased to be when Parliament was dissolved on 8 February. The Labour Party, you will remember, was placing before the electorate a manifesto, the implementation of which would certainly have taken Britain out of the European Economic Community again. So it seemed to me that I had to say to the electorate, 'You now have a choice, and if you value the choice which parliamentary elections give you, then you will use it by taking at face value what you are offered.'"

It was later the same year that Mr Powell did something else that many people found extraordinary. He accepted an invitation to stand as the Unionist member for South Down in Northern Ireland.

"The Ulster Unionists came to me and said: 'You supported us and helped us during the last Parliament when you didn't need to. Now we're in a hung Parliament, with great opportunities open to us. You won't leave us now, will you?'"

Enoch Powell wouldn't. The loyal soldier went to Northern Ireland and served as the member for South Down for thirteen years, until the election of 1987. He was then seventy-five years of age. To some, he remains a sort of demon king: to others, he is held in affection as a sage. Do people, I asked him as we came to the end of the programme, have the wrong impression of him?

"People, and particularly children, react quite favourably to me. I get on well with children, and they evidently get on well with me."

And at home? How would his family describe him — as the old tyrant, the doting grandfather, or both?

"Tyrant, they could not have thought me to be. If there is a tyranny in our household, it doesn't come from the father's side. No, I don't believe that, in retrospect, my two daughters will regard me as having been overbearing."

"And how would your wife describe you?"

"There must be adequate reasons for tolerating someone, as she has tolerated me, for thirty-seven years. There must be some compensations."

The compensations of wit, no doubt, of intellectual prowess, and of conviction — though I can imagine the difficulties of living with someone whose sense of duty is so strong.

He didn't need another book. The Bible and Shakespeare were quite sufficient, he said — as long as he could have the Old Testament in Hebrew and the New Testament in Greek. It goes without saying that it was a piece of Wagner that he chose as the one record he preferred above the others.

For a luxury, he wanted a fish smoker. He has a passion for smoked fish.

15

But then, Enoch Powell has a passion for many things. They are, however, the things of life. I could see that no matter how stirring the Wagner, how uplifting the Greek and how succulent the smoked fish, he would find life alone difficult to bear. For whom would he construct those elegant sentences? With whom would he debate the issues that matter? Whatever his achievements and failures, Mr Powell has always been someone with something to say. To be fulfilled, he has to have another person to whom he can say it.

Enoch Powell

'Entry of the Gods into Valhalla' from *Rheingold* (Wagner)

'Siegmund's Spring Song' from *Die Walküre* (Wagner)

'Siegfried's Forging Song' from *Siegfried* (Wagner)

'Renunciation of Siegfried' from *Twilight of the Gods* (Wagner)

Symphony No. 6, 'Pastoral' (Beethoven)

Symphony No. 9, 'Choral' (Beethoven)

Prisoners' Chorus from *Fidelio* (Beethoven)

'In Native Worth and Honour Clad' from *The Creation* (Haydn)

Book: The *Old Testament* (in Hebrew) and the *New Testament* (in Greek)

Luxury: *A fish smoker*

JOAN COLLINS

Joan Collins' career may depend on her image, but her survival is due to knowledge of herself. Gloss and glamour are her trademark but she has a healthy understanding of the real value of such things. She enjoys them, of course – and makes sure we do too. But at the same time she treats them for what they are – the tools of her trade, not the stuff of life.

Away from the cameras she didn't wear full makeup or stunning clothes. She was chic but casual and, above all, natural. Everything she said – about her relationship with her father, her first glimpse of Hollywood or her marriages – was both honest and perceptive. She has a great sense of humour, and we laughed a lot throughout the interview. She told me she'd like to play more comic rôles – something which, in my inexperienced judgement, she would do very well indeed.

Interviews with big stars can sometimes disappoint. Only when they feel confident enough to give of themselves do they really work. Joan Collins has that confidence. Tucked up in a scruffy radio studio, she giggled and chatted her way through an exhilarating life and emerged at the end triumphant.

"Life is short and life is sweet — it's not going to be sweet
if you're saddled with some man who makes you sick."

On screen Joan Collins is famous for playing rôles that make her appear voluptuous and ruthless. On her desert island she would be altogether different. Alexis Carrington of *Dynasty* may have been a dangerous predator, but her creator has few of the same characteristics. "I don't think I could kill," she told me, "and I couldn't hunt." Even so, the island held many attractions for her. "I'm completely hopeless. I do not belong in the electronic society. I can't even work an oven because I find it all terribly complicated. I probably would do better on a desert island because it's just simplicity."

So it was a back-to-nature Joan Collins who started the programme, climbing trees, finding berries and catching fish. She would listen to music too. "I would probably have it on all the time – although I would love to listen to the sound of the sea. But when I wasn't listening to that, I would play one of my wonderful eight records."

Joan Collins grew up in a theatrical family. Her father was an agent and his mother was a dancer back at the turn of the century. Granny Collins worked with a group called The Three Cape Girls who used to do the can-can around the Cape in South Africa. Joan's aunts were also dancers – with Jack Buchanan and his young ladies. There was something inevitable, therefore, about Joan Collins' choice of career – but she managed to stave off the final decision until she was nine. Before that she had become addicted to a television programme called *Dick Barton – Special Agent*. "I decided I had to be a detective and perhaps get on Dick's team with Jock and Snowy. I got a detective kit and used to go round fingerprinting people all over the house." Luckily for her fans, Joan Collins, sleuth, was a phase which passed. "The more that I went to the theatre, the more I decided I wanted to be an actress."

London was her main home at this time, presided over by her mother. "Mummy was very beautiful and loved clothes and very nice, pretty things. But she wasn't glitzy. She was glamorous – but she was very much a mother. She wasn't interested in anything at all other than her husband, her three children, and running her home as well as she possibly could. She was a very good rôle model in some ways. Of course, I didn't follow it." What she did follow was a life which took her away from home a great deal. She was evacuated to various places in the West Country and the South of England – "I think that's where my gypsy existence came from." It was obviously quite an unsettled life and one which prevented her from being spoiled. "We didn't have sweets, we hardly ever had any fruit, and we were lucky to have sugar and milk. So I grew up eating everything on my plate – which I still do." Here she laughed: "The constant battle of the bulge!"

Joan Collins' childhood relationship with her father was something that mattered to her very much. "There was that thing that little girls have in Anglo-Saxon countries of always trying to get the love of the father, and the father being rather a distant, aloof, strict, patriarchal figure."

Her parents yearned for a son. Instead they had Joan and then her sister, Jackie. Joan tried to compensate. "Daddy used to love to go to football games, Arsenal being his particular favourite. So I used to go along to these games at the age of eleven or twelve, wrapped in a scarf, waving a ratchet, freezing cold, bored to tears, but thinking that he would really approve of me for doing it."

But he didn't. Shortly afterwards, Joan's brother was born and everything changed. I asked her whether she'd ever felt able to please her father and whether he, for his part, had ever found the time to praise or compliment her. "He wasn't that sort of man. He was one of those men that are – not cold, necessarily – but not loving and emotional." It wasn't the "done thing", she said, to give people compliments and she admitted that she still found it difficult to become involved in that way herself and to analyse life. "I find that very American. I've never really been able to do it. I just sort of get on with it." Here, I thought, was where the pop psychologists would jump in, saying that that's what Joan Collins had been looking for in her husbands ever since – the father figure who would be warm where her own father had been cool. "Oh yes," she replied breezily, "but pop psychology has got an answer to every single problem." One of the things that her relationship with her parents *did* do, however, was prevent her becoming like her mother who lived "under my father's thumb". She didn't see herself "getting down and being like Mummy, much as I admired and loved her. I just didn't see the thrill in shopping and cooking and cleaning the house and looking after three brats."

Turning her back on domesticity and all its chores, Joan Collins went off to RADA. It was at this time that she discovered she was deeply desirable to men and adopted a uniform for the purpose.

"I tried to look like somebody called Juliette Greco, who was then very dark with very long black hair, and a long fringe. So I copied that. I had a very long fringe so you couldn't see my eyes, which were covered all round in black eyebrow pencil and I wore black polo-neck sweaters and black stockings and black ballet shoes and big skirts – or very short tight skirts. I also had tons of bracelets. Nothing's changed really," she added with a laugh. "I had huge gold earrings and a sort of sultry look. I used to go down to 100 Oxford Street and dance to Humphrey Lyttelton and George Melly would sing."

Thus dressed and thus occupied, Joan Collins decided that she would make her own way in the world. No man was going to rule her life. It's a decision to which she has stuck – although she admits that in later life "it would have been wonderful to have been able to marry somebody who was on an equal footing financially. Unfortunately it didn't happen."

What did happen was that the young Joan Collins was spotted by a photographer looking for an innocent young face to appear in "a beauty queen film" called *Lady Godiva Rides Again*. It was the start of a whole new way of life for the young RADA pupil whose teachers rapidly tired of her extra-mural activities as a model and would-be film star. When she was offered a rôle playing a good-time girl in the film *I Believe in You*, they refused to give her the twelve weeks' leave of absence she needed. Joan decided then and there to leave RADA and pursue her film career. "I went and did various films for various people and I always played this 'bad girl' rôle." Bad girls, it seems, did well in the cinema of those days. What Ealing Studios had discovered, Hollywood decided it wanted for its own. Howard Hawks was making a film called *Land of the Pharaohs* in Rome – and suddenly needed an actress. It turned out to be Joan Collins' big break, and she told me how it came about.

"It was an American film and they cast a girl to play the wicked Princess Nellipha, but apparently stardom had gone instantly to her head and she started going round telling Howard Hawks and Jack Hawkins what to do. She thought she was the second coming of Grace Kelly and so she was fired immediately. They then called me, whom they'd seen in a few British films and off I went, winging my way to Rome. It was divine in those days. It was the height of *la dolce vita*. There were thousands of American stars over there. So I did this film and then Twentieth Century-Fox saw it and bought me from the Rank Organisation, which was quite amusing. I was bought – like a pound of Brussels sprouts."

By this time Joan Collins was just twenty years old. She arrived in Hollywood when it was entering its last great days. It thrilled her. "It was still a time of true glamour, of wonderful restaurants, of amazing night-clubs, of glorious premières, a time when the press still had a certain amount of respect for stars and celebrities, and, so, consequently, stars and celebrities 'went out', 'dressed up', 'had a wonderful time'. I met within the first week I was there – Gene Kelly, Judy Garland, Humphrey Bogart, Frank Sinatra and Marilyn Monroe. It was quite astonishing, I used to just sit with my mouth open in awe."

Not all the great stars were particularly nice to her. For instance, she found Bette Davis "quite intimidating" when she had to act with her in *The Virgin Queen*. It was the second time Miss Davis had played Elizabeth I and on this occasion she had shaved part of her head so she could wear the red wigs which had been designed for her. She was one of those people, explained Joan Collins, "who came from the school of hard knocks. She always had to fight – but I think it probably didn't make her as nice a person as she should be."

Bing Crosby wasn't very nice either – "not nearly as nice as Bob Hope". Here, Joan Collins gave me a little bit of film lore. You can always tell what an actress or actor is like from the crew, she said. "Far be it from me to speak ill of the dead, but the crew did *not* like Bing Crosby when we did *The Road to Hong Kong* together." And why was that? My castaway was diplomatic: "I just think that some people care about other people and some people don't." And that was all she would say.

Although she'd told me earlier that she was not particularly "analytical" about herself, Joan Collins did at this time in her life take up the Hollywood pastime of visiting a "shrink". Friends of hers such as Marlon Brando, Paul Newman and Joanne Woodward had all taken up the habit – "so all of us lesser mortals suddenly realised shrinks were 'it'". She admits that she did learn quite a bit about herself – but gave it all up long ago. The last time she sought professional advice was from a marriage counsellor when her marriage to Ron Kass was breaking up. "But it just really prolongs the agony. Instead of making the decision you think about all the ins and outs – the children and all of those things. We eventually did split up."

I asked Joan Collins a little more about her marriage to Ron Kass. She had written since that as his wife in the early seventies, when she had just had her third baby, Katie, she had enjoyed "almost perfect years". Was that true?

She said it was. "I think that I had reached a time of my life when I had done the career. I don't really consider that I was ever really a star, but I was quite well known and had acted opposite some of the most illustrious people in Hollywood, and I had decided that by that time, although I liked being a star, it wasn't the be-all and end-all of my life. I really wanted to concentrate on having my children, bringing them up and doing a bit of acting if it came along. So we lived in the house in Highgate and I really couldn't have cared less whether I was a star or not. It was only when, for various reasons, we had to leave England and go to America in 1975 that I became less happy."

In the past, Joan Collins has talked about her marriages – she has had four – in a remarkably frank way. She doesn't regret this, just as she doesn't regret the marriages themselves. "I've had a wonderful life with all of the men that I was married to. For the time that we were together it's been absolutely terrific. But I'm of the opinion that if you're with somebody and it's not working – if it's not bringing you happiness – you should get out. Because life's short and life's sweet. And it's not going to be sweet if you're saddled with some man who makes you sick." She doesn't rule out marriage again – "since I've done it four times, it's obviously something I quite like" – but for the moment is happy as she is. She told me when this programme was recorded in June 1989 that "the last year of my life has been the happiest because I have come much more to terms with who I am and what I am. I have the freedom that I haven't had in my whole life before. I'm doing very much what I want to do."

One thing she would still like to do is play comedy parts. She enjoyed her time on *Dynasty* because she spotted that Alexis should be played "with a certain tongue-in-cheek, rather grand, glamorous woman-of-the-world quality". But now that it's over she is anxious to move on. "It's very difficult when you've been associated with a rôle like that to get away from its image. That's why I want to do more comedy because I think I'm quite good at it."

For the last part of our programme together we talked about the physical side of Joan Collins. At the age of fifty she graced the centrefold of *Playboy* magazine. It was, she says, a statement. "I was saying that it's not only a girl of twenty-three who can look good. I was saying to women: 'Look, maybe you can't look exactly like this but you should know that you can look pretty good'." She feels that in this country, and in America, getting older sometimes feels like a crime. But people in their forties or fifties, she thinks, have more wisdom than those who are younger. They deserve to be appreciated. They should be proud of themselves. She remembered that when she came into the business of acting in her teens she was told that she would be washed up by the time she was twenty-three. "I remember thinking that that was so unfair and wrong, and that it wasn't going to happen to me. Life isn't easy – but you bloody well make the best of what cards you've got to play and play them as well as you can."

That could be Joan Collins' motto. Her great achievement is that she has survived, that the actress who was sought after in her twenties is still at the top in her fifties. To manage that you need not only professionalism, but self-knowledge too. As she herself told me: "I have a sort of enthusiasm for life and I don't ever want to lose it. I like my life. I like who I am and what I do and I'm quite at peace with myself."

She chose moisturiser as her luxury – "because if I didn't have that I would probably turn into a prune very rapidly" – and *The Picture of Dorian Gray* by Oscar Wilde as her book. So with any luck, once rescued, she would return to civilisation in the same delightful condition as when she left it. She deserves that. I think we do too.

Joan Collins

Come Back to Sorrento – Luciano Pavarotti
We'll Meet Again – Dame Vera Lynn
The Wonder of You – Elvis Presley
Come Fly With Me – Frank Sinatra
Intermezzo from *Manon Lescaut* (Puccini)
All I Ask of You (*Phantom of the Opera*) – Steve Barton
and Sarah Brightman
'O mio babbino caro' from *Gianni Schicchi* (Puccini)
Love Will Conquer All – Lionel Richie

Book: *The Picture of Dorian Gray* (Oscar Wilde)

Luxury: *A large bottle of moisturiser*

STEPHEN FRY

We must have made a curious pair. Stephen Fry was wearing his motorbike gear – leather jacket, scarf, and carrying a large helmet. I had just come from some posh function and was dressed up to the nines in a rather expensive outfit. Did I, enquired Stephen Fry solicitously, always dress like this for *Desert Island Discs?* I told him no, and explained the reason for my costume. He seemed relieved. I had the impression that he was beginning to think he ought to go home and change.

There was a lot of tube-train trouble in the bowels of Broadcasting House that day. We had to keep interrupting the recording because of distant rumbles. But Stephen Fry coped with this too. I think the acoustic eccentricities of BH appealed to his sense of the absurd and he seemed to enjoy the whole experience. I hope so, because I certainly did. He's a great talker and his words came thick and fast – faster in fact than with most people. As every radio producer knows, the average rate of human speech is about three words a second. Stephen Fry trots them out at eight words a second.

I suppose some people might argue that he's still too young to be a castaway. It's sometimes said that we should only invite on to the programme people who can look back over a long span of achievement or experience. I don't agree. I think the programme needs to reflect all kinds of different people who make up our way of life, young as well as old. You only have to meet Stephen Fry to be aware that his multiplicity of talents means that he's going to be around for a long time to come. He is part of a whole modern group of people who have refreshed the world of entertainment with their new approach. He certainly earned his place on the desert island – and I don't think anyone who heard his edition of the programme would doubt this.

All eight of his records contained the human voice. Without it, he said, he couldn't exist. So our conversation was punctuated by great singing from a wide variety of people – from Hans Hotte to Meatloaf, from Frank Sinatra to The Bonzo Dog Doo-da Band. Stephen Fry's taste is like his talent. It shows great range.

mind. I can sit any exam and do well. It's a pastichey sort of mind really – I could copy other people's modes of speech and expressions. I don't suppose I ever actually sat down and thought about anything until I was about nineteen. My father knew that: he knew that my academic success, such as it had been, all depended on flair. I never actually thought and I never actually worked."

I was surprised by Stephen Fry's frank appraisal of his youth. He had contempt for his behaviour and contempt for his mind too. The person who had impressed him least, it seemed, was himself. I found this surprising because the person sitting in front of me in the recording studio seemed very different from the embryonic monster he had just described. He appeared modest, charming and approachable – a thoughtful, talented man who deserved his success. Was he wrong in the assessment of his own personality – or had he changed since then?

He talked about something which had a great influence on his life. At the age of seventeen he got into serious trouble and ended up in prison. Stephen Fry talks about this time – as he does about most aspects of his life – in an unassuming way. He hates making what he describes as "a heavy social point", but he acknowledges that it was a turning-point. "There is something faintly distasteful about someone using criminality as a method of improving his life and coming to terms with himself just because he's been able so easily to afford to step out of it in the way that I was." It was that awareness which made him feel guilty – and eventually persuaded him to settle down and go to Cambridge. A less clever and sensitive person might not have reacted in such a positive way.

He was sent to prison after he had run away from his school in Norfolk and gone to London. There he "appropriated" a wallet containing some credit cards and, in his own words, "went ape around five or six counties in Britain, spending wildly on hotels and suits and pointless things like that". He was caught by a receptionist at a hotel in Swindon who, unlike the previous recipients of his custom, had the intelligence to question why a boy with very shabby shoes should have such a plethora of plastic credit. He was given two years' probation, but spent two months in prison while the police sorted out his case.

He got on very well with his fellow prisoners and found it "absurdly easy" to adjust to the whole experience. He had been at boarding school since he was seven and was better able to cope with life in captivity than some of the more hardened inmates. "It was strange how much easier it was for me to adapt to something like that."

Talk of prison and captivity led us naturally to solitude and life on the desert island. "I don't like loneliness but I don't mind being solitary from time to time – as long as I have a sort of control over it. As long as I know there's a telephone – or that I can go round and see someone." He likes his friends – and has many of them. Relationships, however, are altogether more difficult. He prefers to stand apart, leading a celibate life. He's talked in the past about why he doesn't choose to take a sexual partner – and explained for my benefit how this information had first been revealed:

"It happened because some years ago someone from *The Tatler*, in the way they do, had the jolly idea of a series of articles for the Christmas edition on 'Things People Don't Do'. They rang me up on the off-chance that there might be something I didn't do and said 'so-and-so doesn't drive' and he's writing about that, 'so-and-so doesn't watch television' and 'so-and-so doesn't go on holidays' – 'Is there anything you don't do?' And I thought a bit, and scratched my head, and thought: I do almost everything. Then I said: 'Oh, well I don't have sex, is that an interesting one?' And they said: 'What, what, what?'"

I wasn't surprised: it is not the kind of answer the average journalist on a simple Christmas errand would expect. Stephen Fry's view of sex is, perhaps predictably, a little more sophisticated than a renunciation of the whole idea. "One of the reasons I don't like sex is because so often one sees people losing friendship. I think 'liking' is such a tremendous human quality. Often people who love each other don't like each other. That's when it always gets very sad."

The other revelation he had once made about himself was that he is "90 per cent gay". He explained that he'd said it in answer to a question about his life at Cambridge. "I said I had been, I suppose, 90 per cent gay then – and now, being celibate, I would reserve the right not to go to bed with people of either sex. It's an important right."

Stephen Fry won a scholarship to Cambridge. Once again he found himself surprised. He thought it was going to turn out to be a mistake – that he'd get to university and discover they'd muddled up his name with someone else's. But his academic prowess was as genuine as his adolescent insecurity and he enjoyed a university career in the company of people with whom he still performs – such as Emma Thompson, Hugh Laurie and a whole generation of young Footlights players. It was with Hugh Laurie that he wrote a review which won the first Perrier Award at the Edinburgh Festival. I asked him which he preferred – performing or writing? His answer was typically analytical.

"I sort of prefer the one I'm not doing and that's not as arch as it might sound. When you're writing, you do envy actors the fact that they're bossed about – they're told when to go and rehearse, they know when they have to be in the theatre and they know when they have to do everything. They don't wake up in the morning thinking, 'Oh, I've got to write this, how am I going to do this?' Then, when you're acting, you envy writers their freedom. You're there every night at the theatre or you're forced from pillar to post, while a writer can say 'Well, I think I'll do the writing this evening', or 'I'll go out tonight'. They can at least make their own timetable."

Guilt and worry accompany Stephen Fry in a lot of what he does. He's constantly afraid that he's going to be "found out", a feeling which, he told me, he believed was very common in men. I assured him that women suffered from it too! Nevertheless I wanted to ask him why a man with such a natural talent should find himself worrying so much of the time.

"It is one of the world's great cheats really. When you're a child, adults are constantly telling you that there are no short cuts and work is the only thing. Then you grow up – and just as you think, 'I've put the final full stop in my last exam' or 'That's the last essay I have to hand in', you discover that life is actually full of worse exams and worse essay crises than you ever had when you were at school."

He is, he said, meticulous in order to stop himself from not being meticulous, and hard-working to prevent himself from being lazy. He drives himself against his natural grain, pouring his money into cars and computers and, occasionally, shirts. Why shirts? "That's partly because of a sense of physical embarrassment. I think if one can draw attention to the top bit" – that means shirts and pullovers – "it disguises the shape a bit. So people don't look for the ridiculous long legs and the pointless stoop and so on."

His energy and his talents for many different things have drawn criticism from some people, who feel he may be spreading himself too thin. It isn't something he feels he needs to worry about. "The only thing one can do is what one believes in at the moment. I've no particular sense of 'I must stop all this and write plays' or 'I must forget all this writing nonsense and just be in situation comedies'. I haven't really come to any decision. I have no sense of future at all – next week or in two years' time." It's a feeling which extends to his personal life as well. Except in one regard.

"I would like to have a family, which is outrageous really because I'm aware that there are emotions that have to be gone through in order to have such a thing. Obviously no woman would wish to be joined to someone as selfish as me. That's why I long, in a naughty and very wrong way, for a sort of Victorian arranged marriage in which, you know, you come home to a wife and three little moppets and you don't have to . . . don't have to work at it, and so on. But I know that's bad."

Not only bad, I said, but unlikely too. He agreed – and admitted that it made him sad. "I would like the idea of having children. I enjoy godchildren and friends' children very much and there'll always be pleasure in that. It isn't quite the same – but it's better than one might imagine."

The sense of resignation implicit in that remark contrasted with something else that I'd heard about Stephen Fry. I'd read that his friends regarded him as unpredictable – liable to flee the country tomorrow, never to be heard of again. He protested at this, and said he found it difficult to be thought of in that way. And then he seemed to realise what his friends might mean. "I do occasionally get restless," he admitted, "but not necessarily filled with a wanderlust. I need to change myself somehow. This year I suddenly bought a motorcycle and for the first time in my life used aftershave. They're insignificant details in themselves – but a year ago I'd never have thought I'd be the kind of person to wear aftershave." He did it, he said, because he wanted to escape what was beginning to annoy him. He no longer wanted to be a tweedy person in brogues and green corduroys. Now he wears leather jackets.

"So," I enquired, "you don't like being called a gentleman, but you wouldn't want to be called a slob either?"

"No." The reply was gentle but firm. "I'd like to be called Stephen." A Stephen who doesn't like labels and won't be pushed into easy definitions of his work, or his personality. He admits that it's useful to be given an image sometimes – "alternative comedian", if not true in all respects, is at least valuable in allowing the audience to give him an identity – but he prefers to keep himself free of being typecast.

In this he's following the tradition of a man he greatly admires, John Cleese. "He is the God. Everyone can see in him straight away that this man ought to be a barrister – and somehow he isn't. That's what's so wonderful about the way he does everything."

I couldn't ask him to do Cleese's silly walk – which he is known to do extremely well – so we moved instead to his book and his luxury. The book was an omnibus edition of P. G. Wodehouse's Jeeves stories, which provided him "with the greatest pleasure I have ever gained from reading". The luxury, however, was rather less light-hearted. He wanted a suicide pill.

"I know that sounds terrible but I would urge you to believe that in fact it's a very optimistic thing to want to take. I think the fact that I couldn't be on my own shows that I'm reasonably happy with other people and I think it's a great compliment to society that I enjoy it so much that to be banned from it would be a kind of death for me. I'd be much happier to put the final scene from *Götterdämmerung* on my little record player and hear Brünnhilde riding into the flames while I sank slowly into oblivion, quite cheerfully. That would be my luxury. Is that allowed?"

I had to allow it. After all, it didn't have any constructive use. It was a suitably ironic way in which to end our conversation. In Stephen's Fry's world, some things are exactly as they seem. His great talent is spotting those which are not. His rueful eye accepts the obvious and singles out the subtle which is why I hope he would refrain from taking that suicide pill. His account of life on the desert island would be one of the most entertaining we were ever likely to hear.

Stephen Fry

Champagne Aria from *Don Giovanni* (Mozart)
Shirt – Bonzo Dog Band
'Non più andrai' from *The Marriage of Figaro* (Mozart)
I've Got You under My Skin – Frank Sinatra
Bat Out of Hell – Meatloaf
Magic Fire Music from *Die Walküre* (Wagner)
Quartet from *Rigoletto* (Verdi)
'Liebestod' from *Tristan and Isolde* (Wagner)

Book: *The Jeeves Omnibus* (P. G. Wodehouse)

Luxury: *A suicide pill*

ROBERT RUNCIE, ARCHBISHOP OF CANTERBURY

"Is this religious enough, do you think?" enquired His Grace, the Archbishop of Canterbury, halfway through the recording of his programme. It was not an irreverent question – even though it was designed to make us laugh. It's just that Robert Runcie's deep convictions have not dislodged his sense of humour. Nor has his ability to relax undermined his innate presence.

Being the Archbishop of Canterbury must be one of the most difficult jobs in Britain. It's a highly exposed position. With so many people having so many different expectations of you – how on earth are you supposed to behave? I would say – as a humble observer of these things – that this archbishop has behaved very skilfully indeed. He took his shoes off to do the recording. As he padded around our studio in his socks, his large crucifix slapping gently against the purple material of his cassock, his informality struck me as a great strength. He was, I thought, serious without being pompous, warm without being affable, and devoted to his beliefs without being pious or superior – the right characteristics for a man of God in a confused-about-God age.

"My luxury rocking chair – I wouldn't go anywhere
without it."

Knowing where to begin is one of the biggest problems you face when interviewing an archbishop. I was anxious to establish as quickly as I could whether any tension existed between being a religious leader and an ordinary man. After all, the position of Primacy demands a certain distance – even remoteness – while the duties and pleasures of an ordinary man often require the complete opposite. So, right at the start, we discussed this contrast. Could he, I asked, go on sunny holidays? And to emphasise the point, added: "Can an archbishop slip into his bathing drawers on occasions?"

"Oh yes," was the immediate answer. But then: "It's a matter of seeking anonymity." Obviously an archbishop on the beach has to tread a little carefully. He can't simply flop around like the rest of us. Dr Runcie explained his discreet seaside manoeuvres.

"In Kent, where I like to be beside the sea sometimes, I have a friend who is ready to come to Dymchurch beach with me. We go to the waterside, with me in a straw hat and dark glasses, then I quickly whip off the straw hat and the dark glasses and make for the sea, and he's waiting with a towel when I come out."

His Grace also has to be careful about his music. "I'm married to a professional musician and therefore I have an inferiority complex on the subject." However, the Runcies, as you might expect, are nothing if not ecumenical about such matters. "We've come to an agreement about what irritates her and what irritates me." It transpired that although Dr Runcie has grown to love his wife's piano-playing, she does not respond with the same enthusiasm to his singing.

"It's rather alarming," he told me. "Sometimes at a great liturgical service at Canterbury Cathedral, with the place packed, I will start a sursum corda – and I see my wife's hands – which *appear* to be covering her face in prayer – immediately assume that tense indication that her face is being covered in horror."

"There goes that dreadful voice again!" I said, imagining the hidden embarrassment of the Archbishop's wife.

"There goes that dreadful voice again!" he repeated, agreeing that I had captured Mrs Runcie's feelings exactly. She is not alone either. "This is shared, I'm sorry to say, by my family."

Robert Runcie was born in Liverpool – "a very happy household – my mother was romantic, affectionate, dreamy, and my father was an engineer, very Scottish, and very much a man's man – good company, loved sport, and I adored him."

His mother was a hairdresser – "She had this wonderful romantic view of the world, quite a lot of the dreamy side of my mother has probably come into me. Anything that is more masculine, I think has come from my father."

One aspect of this masculinity which undoubtedly missed Runcie *fils* completely was his father's disdain for parsons.

"My father was a marvellous character. He was brought up on Burns and tended to think that you should be wary of people who were in Scottish 'hunkergoode'. He thought that parsons tended to be hypocrites, and the first recollection I have of hearing the name of the Archbishop of Canterbury was when, on the wireless, I heard a voice droning on and my father said, 'That's the Archbishop of Canterbury – unctuous old beggar'."

I didn't dare ask, but I couldn't help wondering, whether old Mr Runcie had really used the word 'beggar'. I suspected a case of self-censorship, prompted by the combined pressures of high office and Radio 4. Nevertheless, his father's strictures cannot have been that serious, for in his teens Robert Runcie found himself drawn towards the Church. Admittedly, the pull was not entirely spiritual.

"A friend of mine at school and I were both keen on the same girl who went to the local school, so when we heard that she was going to confirmation classes, we thought we'd go along too, and I have to say, that's how it all started. Her name was Betty – and I'd better not give it all away . . . she didn't subsequently figure in my life at all, but she was the unknown agent of my being led into the way of religious orthodoxy."

The young Runcie was very keen on jazz and thought that if he couldn't become a cricketer or a football player, it would be good to be in a jazz band. His parents can never have imagined that their son would go on to hold the office he did today.

"They would have been astonished, but they would have been proud, because they would have thought I did what I wanted to do, and I'd achieved something. My father, although he was a little anxious about my religiosity, didn't attempt for one moment to prevent it. It was a home of love and freedom and great expectations, but no forcing, and that's why I think I've had one of the greatest of gifts, which is a happy, secure childhood."

Sadly, neither of his parents lived even to see their son ordained. Dr Runcie's mother died a few months before her son took his orders on Christmas Eve, 1950. "My father became ill when I was in my teens and he lost his sight, and that was an upsetting time in the life of the family. It was happening just when I was coming to exams and playing in the first team, which he would have loved to have seen. He used to come along with my mother faithfully, and she used to try and describe the game, but as she couldn't understand it, she used to get very mixed up and he would get rather irritated.

37

"I used to read the paper to him. He was a great racing man, and with his blindness, of course, this was something that he could do. He could have a little flutter each day and so I used to read the racing page and the form and became quite knowledgeable. Even now, although I don't indulge in it, I always try to boast to my family that a quick look at the sports pages before the National or the Derby would enable me to identify at least one of the first three."

First jazz, now gambling — what next helped to form the character of England's Primate? It was the war, and the Scots Guards. Dr Runcie had said when he was interviewed by the army that he would like to join a Scottish regiment — but he had never thought of the Scots Guards because he believed it to be too expensive. The army told him that in wartime you didn't need much money. So he joined — and went on to win the Military Cross. Would he care to describe what he did?

"Not much," he said. But on *Desert Island Discs* you have to tell stories of this kind, even if you don't want to. For the person telling them, they must be so familiar as to be almost boring — but for the audience at home they sound completely fresh, providing an insight into the life and character of the castaway. Dr Runcie won his MC for two acts of bravery. On one occasion he rescued a fellow soldier from their tank when it caught fire ("That wasn't, as it turned out, too difficult," he remarked, his voice reaffirming his modesty); on another occasion he took his tank out into the open to knock out one on the German side which was holding up the British advance. "I didn't realise how exposed it was." He also didn't realise that he'd done anything particularly courageous. His own memories of the day were, and are, rather different from others'.

"I think that what I remember most, because I hadn't imagined that it was an act that would win any decoration, was walking over to that tank which we'd knocked out about two or three hours later, and seeing the four dead Germans inside — and that did turn my tummy over, and made me think, well, what's it all about? They look just the same as us."

None of Runcie's colleagues at that time apparently had any idea that he might eventually take holy orders. Why did he keep it such a secret, when he was so close to them, fighting by their side?

"It isn't true that nobody had *any* idea, but it wasn't common knowledge. They knew that I turned up when there was an opportunity to go to a service. I hadn't made up my mind finally, and I didn't until after I'd returned to Oxford, but I suppose a little bit of it was . . . cowardice."

One of Runcie's commanding officers was William Whitelaw. Runcie believes the whole Mess would have doubled up with laughter if they'd been told that one day he would be Archbishop of Canterbury and Whitelaw would be Home Secretary.

"The group of men that I soldiered with, the Guardsmen, the gunners, and the drivers of the tank and so on, came together for a little party when I became archbishop. I hadn't seen so many of them for years and they were wonderful, and I remember one of them grasping me by the arm as I left, everybody having drunk my health and wished me well, and he said (here, the Archbishop adopted a broad Glaswegian accent): "Don't worry, sir, if anyone ever says a word about that Hogmanay we spent in Cologne, I'll break every bone in their body."

After the war, Runcie returned to Oxford where he picked up a First in classics, philosophy and ancient history. "I think I surprised people who were my contemporaries when I got a First more than I surprised my fellow officers when I became ordained."

After Oxford, he trained for the ministry in Cambridge and served first as a curate in Tyneside, then went back to Cambridge where, as Dean of Trinity Hall, he met his future wife Rosalind.

"My father-in-law was then the senior fellow of the college and I was the junior fellow, so the junior fellow married the senior fellow's daughter – I think that's called 'endogamy' – marriage within the tribe."

Four years after his marriage Runcie was back near Oxford, this time as Principal of Cuddesdon Theological College. He and his wife were very happy there. With the disciplines of teaching went the duty of being vicar of the local country parish, so the family lived in a country vicarage and the future archbishop was able to indulge his fascination for pigs. Unfortunately, it is a fascination we were unable to explore. Before coming on the desert island he had made a vow: "I promised my family I will not go on about my pigs."

The Runcies spent ten years in Oxfordshire before he moved on to become Bishop of St Albans. He felt he had been at Cuddesdon long enough and the idea of moving halfway between Oxford and Cambridge appealed to him. "I have been fortunate in finding that each step I've taken has brought me to a work which I felt, you know, was right and God wanted me to do."

"Were you aware then that you were in line for Archbishop of Canterbury?"

"People mentioned this, but I never took it seriously, to be honest about it. I remember the night that I received the letter from the Prime Minister. I'd been to a wonderful party, at the BBC as a matter of fact. We came back late and my chaplain, in his dressing gown, handed me an envelope which had 'From the Prime Minister' on it. It had been delivered by motorbike so he had his suspicions, and he said, somewhat solemnly to me, 'Now your troubles begin'."

"Do you think Mrs Thatcher might have some regrets now about having asked you?"

"I have a good friendship with the Prime Minister, who was at Oxford with me, and I was once on one of her committees, and whatever may happen officially we have a very good friendship, but I never presume to ask her that embarrassing question."

"Have you ever regretted accepting the job?"

"Well yes, I think that there have been times but they've been overcome. Life is quite hectic for an archbishop, you know, but those who know me best sometimes say, 'But you really enjoy it, don't you?'"

"And you do?"

"I suspect they may be more right than I admit."

We had come via Liverpool, jazz, the army, country life and (albeit briefly) pigs to the throne of Canterbury. Its position in the established order of English life may still be magnificent, but its influence and power is no longer what it was. We often hear complaints that the Church is not 'spiritual' enough, that it is too involved in politics and that it should spend more time inculcating its flock with religious principles than worrying about their living conditions. We tend to forget that it was an Archbishop of Canterbury, William Temple, who coined the phrase 'welfare state' in 1941. The Church, in our modern society, has made great efforts to integrate with the people rather than stand apart from them. And yet church-going is declining. Why?

"Obviously I would like more followers. But I think that there is often uncertainty on moral issues. What it is possible for people to choose to do is greatly multiplied and the Church has tended to look rather quarrelsome, rather than creating spiritual energy in the life of the country."

This archbishop has never been afraid of entering the political arena if that's where the voice of Christian conscience has led him. But it does mean he has become a controversial figure at times. In asking whether that surprised him, I received an answer that seemed to crystallise many of his beliefs.

"I have felt that the kind of things that I've been saying spring from my fairly orthodox Christian belief, and a desire to apply that belief to personal and social circumstances and things that I know about. I feel that one of the things that you have to do is to stand up for people who are not sharing, for example, in the general improvement in the wealth of a country – the casualties of affluence, if you like. Mind you, one of the difficulties is that the Church should, quite rightly, support those who have the responsibility to govern. I always think it's symbolic that the bishops sit on the government's side in the House of Lords. It's not that they always vote with the government, but they believe in government as such, and order in society. But then I say that the Church has a duty to be the conscience of a people and to exercise a kind of critical solidarity with government."

This is a central argument as far as the Church in modern Britain is concerned. "There are," says Dr Runcie, "moral issues that lie behind political judgement which must bring anybody who is an official representative of the Church into the public arena. I'm quite unashamed of that."

The Archbishop, as befits a man of intellect, chose Homer's *Odyssey* in Greek as his book – "I could see myself perhaps pacing the sands and reciting the lines of Homer" – and, as befits a man of peace, a rocking chair. But not any old rocking chair. "This one was created in very unluxurious circumstances. When I was in India a very poor community took immense trouble and they made me this lovely rocking chair with basketwork at the back. I wouldn't go anywhere without it. It's my luxury rocking chair."

I can see that it must bring welcome relief from the cares of the throne of Canterbury.

Robert Runcie

'Sea Slumber Song' from *Sea Pictures* (Elgar) – Dame Janet Baker
Dinah – Fats Waller
Regimental March of the Scots Guard (Hielan' Laddie)
Love Duet from *La Bohème* (Puccini)
The Lark Ascending (Vaughan Williams)
'Laudate dominum' from *Vespers*, K339 (Mozart)
In the Bleak Mid-winter – Canterbury Cathedral Choir
'Sanctus' from Mass in B minor (Bach)

Book: *The Odyssey* (Homer)

Luxury: *His own rocking chair*

ERIC CLAPTON

Eric Clapton's edition of *Desert Island Discs* has been the only one I have recorded outside a BBC studio. We had arranged for the programme to be made as usual at Broadcasting House, but the reclusive musician eventually lured me to his country home in the Surrey Downs. It is a magnificent setting – pleasant English tranquillity far removed from the hell-raising life of a rock musician. On the surface Eric Clapton, at forty-four, appears to be a very different man from the one who commanded such a huge following in the sixties when he played with the Yardbirds, Cream and Blind Faith. He's still enormously popular, of course, but age appears to have quietened the roaring style of his youth.

Quietened, perhaps, but not extinguished: in the house which I visited were many of the trappings of a successful career, but the man who had earned them seemed to stand slightly apart from them all. The house was busy. We were met in a nearby village by one of his assistants who guided us through the lanes for the last few miles of our journey. When we got there, gardeners and builders were working outside and Eric Clapton seemed to be surrounded by a bevy of different helpers. He was friendly and welcoming, chain-smoking throughout our conversation, and prepared to answer even the most intimate questions.

But his personal warmth seemed contained within him. It didn't spread throughout his splendid mansion and I had the impression that what Eric Clapton owned was by no means the most important part of his life. He may possess a garage full of Ferraris, but he is not seduced by them. It is his music which absorbs him and, in a sense, isolates him too.

I was surprised – and pleased – by Eric Clapton's willingness to be frank about his private life and the drugs and drink he has fought and put behind him. But I was also aware that he had learned to deal with such personal questions in an articulate, nevertheless, elusive, way. He was perfectly prepared because he had already asked the questions of himself.

Some time after this recording, Eric Clapton appeared with his old friend Pete Townshend on a television programme I was presenting. Together they played a blues. It was an unrehearsed moment – exciting in its skill and its warmth. And it confirmed my view that although Eric Clapton may not have led a conventional life, he knows unerringly what he can do and what he loves. It must be this which has sustained him and kept him successful and admired for so long.

"When I was young, it was me and my guitar against
the world."

One of the first things I discussed with Eric Clapton was his luxury. He had assumed that whatever else might be denied him on his desert island he'd automatically have a guitar. Not as something special, but because a guitar is what he always has. I thought it only fair to rob him of this delusion at the beginning of the programme. It must have seemed cruel. To the audiences he entertains so successfully his guitar may simply be the instrument he plays – but to Eric Clapton it is an extension of himself. "When I was young, it was me and my guitar against the world," he told me.

Of the eight records he chose, three reflected important events in Eric's life. He has chosen them for this purpose, using a musician's skill to find pieces that he loved not only for their beauty but for their significance as well. The first was a Puccini aria from one of the composer's less well-known operas, *Suor Angelica*.

"I tend to listen to music which is completely divorced from what I do when I'm working regularly and hard. I love Puccini – I love Italian opera in general – I find it gives me great tranquillity to listen to and it's very moving."

The aria he wanted was 'Senza Mamma', in which the heroine of the opera, a nun called Sister Angelica, laments the news that her illegitimate child, the scandal of whose birth drove her into the convent in the first place, has died. It's music which reminds Eric Clapton of his origins. When we had listened to it I asked him why.

"It's similar in some respects," he said. "My mother left when I was very, very young. I was raised by my grandparents but I didn't know that until I was older." He was nine when he discovered that the couple he thought were his parents were in fact his grandparents.

"The funny thing was that when I heard this piece of music, I had no idea of the story but it had a very profound effect on me. It was only later when I examined the libretto that I discovered it was a very parallel story. I listen to it and I feel what my mother must have felt, the agony of watching me grow from a distance, and not being able to take part in that."

It's hard to imagine the shock of such a discovery. I asked him whether he could remember what it was like to learn such news at such an impressionable age.

"It was very confusing because I knew that I was different, and I didn't know why. I mean I knew that other kids at school regarded me as different, or maybe inferior, and I did have a massive inferiority complex as an adolescent. I chose to conquer it by playing the guitar. It was my haven. Music was my haven in my teenage years."

46

Music gave him strength and was his friend. It was *his*: it belonged to him. But even this could not completely destroy the trauma of what happened to him as a little boy. "It took me a long time to get over it," he explained. "In fact I think it's not properly dealt with yet. It takes you all your life really." Nevertheless he has always got on with his mother extremely well – even if their relationship is rather different from that of other mothers and sons.

"We're more like brother and sister because she was very young when I was born. We're actually just great pals more than anything else. Although I know she still feels that maternal thing – you know."

Eric Clapton's second record related to another significant event in his life. It was opera again, this time the duet from Bizet's *The Pearl Fishers*. He confessed to having first heard it on *Two-Way Family Favourites* when he was a kid. Here again, though, he did not find out the story behind the duet until much later. In fact, it's about two men swearing eternal friendship: both have loved the same woman, but their friendship has survived. The parallel in Clapton's life is his relationship with George Harrison. He told me the story.

"We were friends from the mid-sixties – I did a Beatles show at Hammersmith when I was with the Yardbirds, and we became fast friends. For me it was great to have a friend who was famous and worldly. He was slightly older, so he was a bit like an older brother. He liked me, I think, because of my dedication to the blues and rock-and-roll and we had a lot in common."

Their friendship, however, came under strain when George Harrison married Patti Boyd. Clapton met her and, in his own words, "fell blisteringly in love". It remained unrequited love until, some years later, Patti's marriage to George began to break up. Eric and Patti then began to see each other until she finally left George Harrison. None of this, says Clapton, damaged his friendship with George.

"When I told him about it, George's attitude amazed me. It was, 'Well if that's what's got to be, that's what's got to be. As long as we're still friends, that's the important part.' My love for Patti is still there and always will be. And the love for George has never ever waned."

Eric Clapton married Patti Boyd in 1979. Their marriage ended five years ago but they, too, are still friends and she remains an inspiration for his music: "I don't think it's right to look back and close the door. I've just written and recorded a song which is about being haunted by the spectre of a love that won't die. It's something I live with."

The other record which Eric Clapton chose as a strong reflection of his life was by one of his heroes. "Muddy Waters was, I think, the biggest influence on me in that he seemed to epitomise the consummate blues musician. He was a great person to be able to admire because he wasn't degenerate, he wasn't into dope, he was very straight. He was a tranquil man, almost like a Buddha figure when you met him – and, for me, he was a great person to follow. We worked together and we got on very well. His music was a very strong part of my upbringing."

What Muddy Waters represents, of course, is the exact opposite of the life which Eric Clapton has led. That's why he is significant. So why was it that Clapton failed where his hero succeeded?

"It was a combination of things. I'd always been dabbling with drugs. As a teenager we used to take these things called black bombers, and stay up all night. And I think I smoked a bit of pot during the sixties. But then a combination of events happened – first, falling in love with Patti, and the early hopelessness of that situation, and then losing my grandfather. He died of a stroke, and I started taking heavy drugs within about a month. I see now as I look back that it had a lot to do with the pain of losing this man. I was unaware of the fact that I adored him, as a father figure. Suddenly he wasn't there any more, and I found myself taking heroin."

How did he graduate from cocaine to heroin?

"I was buying cocaine, and the dealer would say, 'I'll sell you some of this but you've got to buy some of this as well', so I would buy this little phial of heroin and put it in a drawer. And I found that after a while I had a drawer full of this stuff and I thought one day: Give it a try. And I did, and I was hooked. I didn't know I was hooked. That's the unfortunate part about drugs. You don't know and you deny all through it. Suddenly you find that if you try and stop, you can't."

Clapton became a total junkie. Hooked on heroin, he became a recluse and shut himself away in his house in Surrey. Eventually he found help.

"Thank God," he says, "I'd never resorted to taking it intravenously because I think that makes it twice as difficult to break the habit." After several weeks of treatment he found he was free of all withdrawal symptoms – but left with a great "spiritual and emotional vacuum". This, he said, "I chose to fill with alcohol."

It is a frightening story. Does he look back and regret what happened?

"I think it's very foolish to do that because you can end up with too much regret. That can be overbearing and make you bitter. I don't particularly relish that time, but it just happened. I can't change the past."

There seems to have been an extraordinary amount of turmoil in Eric Clapton's life. The shock of his childhood discovery, the difficulty of his relationship with his friend's wife, the drugs, and then the alcohol – how many of these things were simply force of circumstances and how many due to his own unpredictable nature? Perhaps, I asked him, he was quite simply one of those people who attracts problems?

"Attracts trouble," he corrected me. "I think you may be right. Even now my private life is in complete chaos. I am stricken with this disease of being ill-content."

This might be interpreted as the familiar cry of the misunderstood artist. To be fair, Eric Clapton won't have anything to do with that. He can't, he said, accept the fact that he needs drugs and drink to be a suffering genius. No: he has a simpler explanation.

"Maybe I never grew up. Now I'm starting to. I wake up every day feeling fresh and a little calmer. But I don't think it will ever resolve. I'm just a kind of wanderer."

Wanderer he may be: but on the concert stage he remains a fixed point that can attract and mesmerise huge audiences. When he plays he appears to transport himself away from his immediate physical surroundings, taking his onlookers with him. I asked him to explain this to me.

"Sometimes time stands still, and I go into a trance-like state. And, from what I hear, I gather that people come with me. There's nothing better on earth for me than being in a concert situation where you can take a whole audience out of themselves for the briefest possible moment. It's a glorious experience when 2,000, 3,000 or 4,000 people, as one, just leave themselves and forget where they are, who they are and just go into this joyous state. It's something that I regard as a great gift."

After that we talked about friends again. Many of his are great musicians like George Harrison, Pete Townshend and Phil Collins. They looked after him when he was deeply dependent on drugs – and even thought of a kidnap to get him away from their source. But Clapton, although he appreciated their kindness, was unable to respond. "Even though they all stood by me," he says, "I still went back to that bloody drug." Drink when it came was an even more powerful attraction. "It was the most important relationship I ever had in a way. More important than my marriage or anything else. They could all have gone to the wall as long as I had the bottle."

Eric Clapton is a father these days. His small son lives with his mother in Italy. He remains in this country – alone in his large country house with his five Ferraris, his collection of wristwatches – and his guitar. He decided he'd take the complete works of Dickens to his island. Ever vigilant, I told him that complete works were not allowed. He would have to choose one.

"*Barnaby Rudge*," he said. "I like the name."

I got the impression that books were not very important to Eric Clapton. He may have led a vivid life and stability may still elude him, but his gift for music is as reassuring a possession as a man could wish for.

"I think for me," he said towards the end of our interview, "the great thing about music is that it is such a great sustenance. I can get nutrition from music in itself – even if I had nothing else." No wonder he needed that guitar.

Eric Clapton

'Senza mamma' from *Suor Angelica* (Puccini)
Duet from *The Pearl Fishers* (Bizet)
Crossroads Blues – Robert Johnson
Feel Like Going Home – Muddy Waters
I Was Made to Love Her – Stevie Wonder
Hard Times – Ray Charles
I Love the Woman – Freddie King
Purple Rain – Prince

Book: *Barnaby Rudge* (Charles Dickens)

Luxury: *A guitar*

JOHN OGDON

John Ogdon died before his programme was transmitted. It was made in June 1989. He died the following August while *Desert Island Discs* was off the air, and so this edition eventually went out a month later as a Radio 4 tribute to him.

John Ogdon's long battle against mental illness has been well recorded. He himself, however, gave very few interviews after it began. *Desert Island Discs* was a perfect opportunity for him. It gave him a chance to present himself as he was – a man irrevocably changed by the terrible difficulties he had experienced but at last in a sufficiently stable frame of mind to perform again and to start to rebuild his interrupted career. Above all, it demonstrated to a wider public what those who were close to him already knew: that his natural talent, his genius even, may have been obscured by psychiatric problems but it could never be extinguished. Throughout the torments of his life, he remained a brilliant musician.

Large, shaggy, rumpled and chain-smoking, John Ogdon cut an unusual figure at the end of his life. His gentle, slightly hesitant voice contrasted oddly with the size of his frame. Often apologetic, he seemed to possess an overwhelming desire to please, as if trying to make amends for the agonies he and those close to him had suffered as a result of his breakdown. But you only have to watch a recording of his victory in the Moscow Tchaikovsky Prize of 1962, or to have seen him on the concert platform towards the end of his life, to realise the volcanic dynamism which lay within. Meeting him, I felt that he had adopted a sort of positive gentleness as if that were the only way in which he could control the forces which had diverted him.

He came to the recording accompanied by his wife, Brenda Lucas, herself a pianist, with whom he gave many concerts and made recordings. I am grateful to her for allowing me to include my interview with John in this book.

"I was tremendously happy playing the piano . . ."

John Ogdon could never lose his love of the piano. At the age of fifty-two he still practised four hours a day and enjoyed it very much. "I hope that in some ways I'm playing a bit better," he told me. Confronted by such happy passion, I decided to begin where I normally finished and asked him straight away if he would have to have a piano as a luxury because he couldn't live without one.

"Well, yes," he confessed. "I think a piano would be a brilliant idea for a luxury."

He had not had much difficulty in choosing the music he wanted for his desert island. "I didn't let too many other thoughts come crowding in," he said. "I simply chose these marvellous pieces." The result was a rich selection of music by composers whom he had known, such as Benjamin Britten and William Walton and pieces played by pianists whom he admired, such as Vladimir Ashkenazy, Daniel Barenboim and Vladimir Horowitz.

John Ogdon was born in Nottinghamshire. His family was very musical. His father wrote one or two essays on Berlioz and played the trombone and xylophone. His mother was a music-lover too, as were his brothers and sisters. Young John first sat at the piano at the age of four. By the time he was eight the family had moved to Manchester and he was talented enough to win a junior exhibition to the Royal Northern College of Music. He could compose, and wrote several sonatas for the piano. His own favourite composer was Rachmaninov, "so tuneful and melodious – beautiful".

The young prodigy could not have been in a better city than the Manchester of the early fifties in which to exercise his talents. He enjoyed Manchester Grammar School, and then went on to the Royal Northern College, which was particularly rich in musical talent at the time, numbering among its students such names as Alexander Goehr, Peter Maxwell Davies and Harrison Birtwistle. "We could all get together in complete freedom." Ogdon was encouraged to enter competitions, and went off to Brussels with the fellow piano student who was to become his wife, Brenda Lucas. He got knocked out on that occasion: the prize went to a young Russian called Vladimir Ashkenazy. But he remained convinced that he was good enough to continue in the intensely competitive world of international piano playing and, in 1962, decided to enter the Tchaikovsky Piano Competition in Moscow. "I'd always been enthused with Russian music," he explained. "My father was enthused with it, and so I felt with this affinity that I ought to enter. You know – have a go at it." The whole experience was one that he remembered with great fondness. "We had a wonderful time. It was very exhilarating and very nerve-racking. There were one or two very good French competitors and, of course, two or three fine competitors from the Soviet Union." He was in Moscow for three weeks, but throughout his stay he never heard any of his rivals play. He did this on purpose. "I thought – really one is trying to play in one's own way, hoping it will come out all right."

As well as Tchaikovsky's first piano concerto, Ogdon played Liszt's Piano Concerto no. 1. "I did feel that it had gone exceptionally well. I felt very happy." Throughout one evening and into the early hours of the next day, the competitors waited to hear the results. When they came they were stunning. John Ogdon and Vladimir Ashkenazy were to share the first prize. It was the first time in the long history of the competition that a British player had won. "I felt really wonderful – but stunned at the same time." Ogdon and Ashkenazy were the same age. They became firm friends – a friendship which lasted throughout Ogdon's life. Of course, there were some who said that Ashkenazy had only been given joint first place because the Russians couldn't bear to give their coveted prize to an Englishman alone. But John Ogdon rejected this when he talked to me. "I think we both played on pretty much top form. I felt very happy with the result. And very honoured."

Victory in Moscow changed John Ogdon's life. At the age of twenty-five, Manchester's prodigy was wanted the world over. The concert circuit became his life. He toured Australia, the United States and Europe. He became very famous; he lived well; he had achieved nearly everything he had ever wanted. "I felt very happy and fulfilled. I think I was tremendously happy playing the piano – and going on the concert tour circuit." Then after ten years of such a life, it all began to go wrong.

"I began to get some depressions over a long period of time. Suddenly they culminated in a nervous breakdown. I felt rather given to irrational moods and not connecting things up properly – you know, words and things." It got so bad that he himself recognised that he would need treatment. In despair, he asked his wife to find help. "I said: 'Please send for a psychiatrist. I think we need one.'" Gently I reminded him that prior to this crucial moment, he had in fact attempted to take his own life. He found it a painful memory. "I'm ashamed to say yes." And then added innocently, "I think one never should."

For the Ogdons, the realisation that John was seriously ill was like a bomb dropping on their lives. Suddenly everyone had to admit that, for the moment at least, his career was at an end. There were to be no more concerts; instead he was admitted to the Maudsley Hospital in South London. He lived there for about eighteen months. His recollection of that time was very touching, almost childlike.

"It was very well organised and regulated and there was plenty of opportunity for recreational activities like painting, listening to music and practising on the hospital piano, which was very kind of them. They sort of arranged it, you know. I practised for about two hours daily." It would have been obvious to anyone why he had been allowed that piano. Whatever his physical and mental condition, the instrument he loved acted as a bridge between confusion and coherence. At the piano, John Ogdon became something like his old self again. I asked him about this, wondering whether he could explain the influence it had over him. "I do feel I light up a bit more, yes. I get very involved with the music. I think it's something to do with the feeling of the keys under the fingers – a sort of tactile feeling that seems to spark things off." But despite the pleasure he felt when he played, he remained fearful that he would never manage to perform in public again. "I had some bad chemical reactions. But I had a lot of help from Brenda – and also quite a lot of help from Gerard Sherman who would listen very carefully for any lack of co-ordination."

Altogether John Ogdon stayed away from the public platform for nine years. He had been desperately ill; he and his whole family had suffered terribly. But by January 1981 he felt ready to try again. He gave a recital at the Queen Elizabeth Hall in London.

"I played the Schumann Symphonic Studies, opus 13, which are tremendously difficult. They're not the most pianistic pieces in the world – but they are very beautiful musically."

And the reaction? Once again, I thought, he became quite childlike. His answer was all innocence and humility: "The audience were very warm and they seemed to receive it very well. I enjoyed it enormously." Which was John Ogdon's way of saying that there was a standing ovation, many encores and, according to some of the critics, the old Ogdon magic was back. "I think I did do about three encores," he finally told me. "They seemed to enjoy it. They were very kind and nice. I did really feel I'd been able to start again."

Inevitably John Ogdon never quite returned to the world he had left behind. For the last years of his life he took a drug to help him maintain mental balance. "I take lithium carbonate," he explained, "which is a blood salt that we have in our blood naturally. This has proved a wonderful stabiliser and it helps to control swings of mood. It also gives you a blood salt that you need biologically as well." The trouble with the drug, he found, was that it had a calming effect. But he tried to overcome this. "I think one has to simply try and get the surge of adrenalin."

He also had a permanent nurse with whom he lived in one flat while his wife lived next door. "Brenda has the basement flat and I have the one on the first floor. We communicate through the telephone a lot, and of course see each other as much as possible. I feel I've had the good fortune after this illness, thanks to Brenda's devotion, to make a good recovery. I love to see my children and we get together whenever we can. Brenda loves to see them too – and we arrange get-togethers as often as possible, at neighbourhood restaurants."

He had one or two pupils – "they're very talented and an inspiration and a joy to teach" – and looked forward to his concerts, hoping one day that he'd be able to play more Mozart. "I'd love to play more Mozart concertos," he revealed. "But I think I've got to improve my Mozart technique first. But I love the pieces."

For his last record, John Ogdon asked for Debussy's 'La Mer' played by the orchestra from the city where he had first learned his music – the Hallé from Manchester under the leadership of their most famous conductor, Sir John Barbirolli. We had already established that his luxury would be a piano – but we made it a little more luxurious by ensuring that it was a Steinway grand. His book was Wilkie Collins' *The Moonstone*.

I felt privileged to have interviewed John Ogdon. It could never be described as the most revealing edition of *Desert Island Discs*. The drugs which calmed him seemed to have numbed him too. His view of his life was hidden behind a cloak of modesty and gratitude; they seemed to be the feelings he used to keep unpleasant realities at bay. But beneath all that – in everything he said and did – there remained an unswerving belief in his own talent. His love of the piano, his knowledge of music and his enjoyment at giving brilliant performances were his partners throughout his life. He was at one with the music which he played and his contribution to the musical life of Britain was enormous. As I said goodbye to him outside Broadcasting House that day, I wondered whether at any point in his life an interviewer would have been able to learn much more about him. His talent was a force buried deep within him. He knew its dangers and its blessings, which is perhaps why only he was chosen as its guardian.

John Ogdon

'Dawn' from 'Four Sea Interludes' from *Peter Grimes* (Britten)
Piano Concerto No. 4 in G minor (Rachmaninov)
L'Ile joyeuse (Debussy)
Symphony No. 1 (Walton)
Piano Sonata in B minor (Liszt)
Tarantella from Suite No. 2 (Rachmaninov) – John Ogdon and
Brenda Lucas
Piano Concerto No. 20 in D minor (Mozart)
La mer (Debussy) – Hallé Orchestra

Book: *The Moonstone* (Wilkie Collins)

Luxury: *A Steinway grand piano*

LESLIE GRANTHAM

It was only when I met Leslie Grantham for the first time that I realised I knew him from somewhere else. Watching him on television I always felt he was familiar. In the flesh, I recognised him as the assistant who used to pin up my skirts in a shop in the Fulham Road in London. He'd worked there for a short time during one of those unusual periods when he was out of work. He was very good at it. He is a man who knows how to make the best of things.

Leslie Grantham agreed to be a castaway as his part in the BBC Television soap opera *Eastenders* was coming to an end. While that was in full swing he was guarded closely. Perhaps that was hardly surprising, given the way the press had treated the revelation that he had once served a prison sentence for murder. During the research for our programme I read through many of the cuttings about the incident and was horrified by the attacks which had been made upon him.

Nevertheless, I knew that if he were to appear on the programme it was an area of his life that we would have to discuss. He had to agree to talk about the murder and his prison sentence. Once again, this reveals an important aspect of *Desert Island Discs*. As a guest on the programme, you cannot simply veto important parts of your life. All you can do is put your own point of view and trust that you will be treated fairly. This is what Leslie Grantham did. The result, I think, was a programme in which a man who had been the subject of considerable vilification was able to put his own point of view at last. He did so easily and confidently, making a programme which proved, if proof were necessary, that the desert island can find a home for everyone in the end.

"If the public want me to play this rather rough, tough,
volatile unstable character – fine!"

Dirty Den' is dead. Long live Leslie Grantham. In the first four years of its existence, Leslie Grantham appeared in nearly every episode of *Eastenders*. He worked six days a week on the set and spent the seventh learning his lines. Playing the part of the unreliable landlord of the local pub, he was on the screen in 410 of the first 418 episodes of the series. Now he's left that arduous world behind to pursue a career which he hopes will prove his versatility as an actor. He doesn't mind if audiences still want to see him in the same type of part. "If the public want me to play this rather rough, tough, volatile, unstable character – fine. It didn't hurt Peter Lorre and it hasn't hurt several other actors." He's glad to be out of *Eastenders* but grateful for the opportunity it gave him. And, as he admits, "the money was nice".

At home, his character is rather different from the image which reaches the screen. He's married with two little boys, Jake and Spike. He cheerfully confesses to being a loving husband and a doting father – exactly the opposite of 'Dirty Den'. "You've got to remember," he told me, "that people do put people in compartments. If you follow the popular press it looks as if everyone just fits into capsules."

He was born in Camberwell in South London in 1947. He had two brothers, one sister, and "lots of mates". People tell him that he was a bit of a lad but at first he claimed not to remember. "I thought I was rather boring really. I didn't even have any girlfriends." I pressed a little. I couldn't imagine that he was a teacher's pet. Here he was happy to concur. "I used to get the cane quite regularly. I remember one incident where I got the cane – I think it was for something I didn't do, which was usually the case – and the deputy head broke his braces while he was giving it to me. When he was leaving I gave him a new pair of braces as a present. I think he was more touched by that than anything else – that this little tearaway whom he used to cane nearly every morning actually should remember the broken braces." Then he paused and finished with a rueful confession: "Yeah – I suppose I was a tearaway."

Leslie Grantham, South London lad, grew up in the swinging sixties, influenced by mods and rockers and developing a bug for performing. "I used to emulate the people on the television. If the Clark Brothers were dancing I would try and do the same – slide across the floor in my pyjamas without ripping my knees."

But, at that stage in his life, a bug for performing could not a career make. His father had been a printer and would have liked his son to become one too, but Leslie did not like the idea. After a spell as a junior laboratory technician – "part of the job was killing horses and I didn't really want to kill horses" – he joined the army. His father, who had served in the Royal Fusiliers, was pleased and so young Leslie felt pleased too. He has, he said, "a great respect and admiration" for his dad. In the army, he was among his own kind, "very much Londoners – although I didn't have that pronounced cockney accent when I was a kid. I think we all wanted to be soldiers when kids." And he appeared to be a good soldier too. "They seemed to think so. They seemed to think I was destined for great things." Which is why, as a teenage recruit in the British army, he found himself serving in Osnabrück in West Germany. It was here one night that an incident took place which was to change the whole course of his life.

It is now widely-known that as a young soldier Leslie Grantham attempted to rob a taxi-driver and, while threatening him with a gun, killed him. He was found guilty of murder and sentenced to life imprisonment. As a result he spent more than eleven years in prison.

It was this central episode in his life that we talked about next. To begin with, I asked him about the background to the crime. Why was he in such desperate need of money?

"Just recently it's become known that there is a lot of bullying going on in the army. Suddenly everyone's got their arms up in the air as if it's something new, just happened overnight, but it's actually been there since the army began. There was a sort of resentment that I was an NCO, and one night this incident happened. There was a lot of what we call – or called – bed-barring, where they take these metal bars off and smash some unfortunate chap across the head. Well, the chap that they were going to do that night wasn't in, but I was in my room and I was burned with a steam iron. I think I went slightly strange."

Blackmail, it seemed, was also part of the bullying. Money could buy off the 'bed-barrers'. So Leslie Grantham found himself in need of cash – and was prepared to rob a taxi-driver to get it. But he told me about these circumstances as a background to what happened, not as an excuse.

"There's no justification for what I did. It's one of the things that I never really talk about. Unfortunately someone lost their life and I spent a time in prison and I don't think that I'll ever have wiped the slate clean. But I think I'm trying to do something with my life. It was a tragic and unfortunate chapter which I'm not proud of and never will get out of my system. It's obviously a very regrettable incident, not just for me, but for everyone involved. But the true story will never come out, and that's maybe a good thing because otherwise it would open up a whole can of worms which should be left buried."

Certainly there was no point in raking over the details of the incident again. Anyway, the murderer had paid his price. Or had he? I didn't ask him outright, but Leslie Grantham volunteered the thought that it just wasn't as simple as that.

"I'm not sure that I paid my price. I still think that being deprived of liberty and punished is some way towards it. But it doesn't wipe the slate clean inside your head. So you still carry on your prison sentence – every day really. I'm just lucky that I've been given the opportunity to start again."

From the age of nineteen to the age of thirty, Leslie Grantham was in prison. He admits he was shocked at the verdict. For his family it was just as terrible. "I think my parents and my family took it worse. I can become detached about things so I can actually shut myself off and overcome it. I had to survive. And my way of surviving is to shut up shop and just go through with a purpose." His detachment – and his sense of purpose – obviously stood him in good stead. Now he can say: "It had to be done. I survived. I came out without too many chips on my shoulder."

I was pleased we had discussed this part of Leslie Grantham's life in the way we had. It is a strength of *Desert Island Discs* that it allows people to put even the most disagreeable of events in the context of their lives and to give them perspective. One incident is not equivalent to one life. Leslie Grantham is the living proof of that.

It was while he was in prison that the bug which had urged him to skid across his bedroom floor finally took hold properly. As a prisoner, he became an actor – and, as actors do, he told an entertaining story about how it all began.

It was the day he was transferred from the boys' wing, where the under-21s were kept, to the men's wing. He had to have a medical inspection but when he reported to the MO, as arranged, he found one man sitting alone outside and two others sitting side by side but some distance away. Leslie Grantham took a chair to sit next to the men who were together.

"The bloke from the other end said, 'Don't sit there, he's got a dose.' I said, 'Pardon?' He says, 'Come and sit here.' So I said, 'What do you mean, he's got a dose?' He said, 'He's got VD' – I thought, Ah, terrible, and he said, 'That's the guy who's given it to him, the other guy sitting next to him.' So I thought, Oh well, have to be careful in here, won't I? Well, that night there happened to be a play on, I think it was called *Norman*, and the play was going through and suddenly the chap with the dose walked on-stage and had to say to this woman, 'But why won't you marry me?' and some of the other prisoners screamed out, 'Because you've got a dose, you idiot.' So I thought, I could do better than this, and someone said to me, 'Well why don't you do it then, why don't you just get up and do it?' So I applied to join the drama group."

It wasn't exactly a leap to stardom, but a beginning all the same. His colleagues in the drama group were, he says, all "the other side of the coin", but Leslie survived and one night when "the leading actor was off having his electric shock treatments" he was asked to take over the main part. After that he appeared in several productions, sometimes with professional actresses who came in from outside to advise and to help fill the cast. From them he received great encouragement, but was suspicious of their motives. "I thought people just felt sorry for you because of the environment you were in," he says. He was also writing plays, but here he had rather a slow start.

"I called it *Comedy of Errors*, not knowing that some other chap a few years before had actually written a play already called *Comedy of Errors*. This was about guys in prison. Everyone read it and thought it was very funny and we thought, right, we'll send this off to someone. And lo and behold, we didn't send it off, but lo and behold, on to the screen came *Porridge*. So that was torn up and thrown out the window."

Eventually, however, he wrote a play which won an award at the Gloucester Festival. He also met the actress Louise Jackson who told him that he should be an actor and so, at last, it dawned that people weren't just being nice after all. Perhaps it was time: he did have talent. He applied for various drama schools – and Webber Douglas took him in. His eleven years in prison were over. How, I wondered, did he react to freedom?

"I'd actually been in an open prison. I used to go to college one day a week and organise the drama group there, and I'd go to the Bristol Old Vic and watch plays. So I'd seen a bit of the world although, obviously, escorted by a prison officer. But I remember, the first day, coming out and going into a shop. And someone said, 'Can I help you?' and I said, 'Yes' and I grabbed something off the shelf and paid for it. It was a tin of cat food. And I thought, Well, I haven't got a cat, really, what do I want this for? – so I wasted 39p on a tin of cat food that I didn't really need."

It seemed a curious reaction to liberty. Why had it happened? Because, he explained, he was confused. In prison when asked a question he had been used to jumping to attention and answering smartly. In a grocer's shop he felt he had to do the same.

It was at drama school that he met Jane Laurie, who was to become his wife, and Julia Smith who became his producer on *Eastenders*. But he doesn't think Julia Smith remembers him from those days. At the end of one production in which he'd been heavily involved, "she went around and said to everyone 'Marvellous, darling, marvellous', and never said a word to me". It did him no harm. Three years later she gave him the part that turned him into a star.

Leslie Grantham believes that the success of 'Dirty Den' owed much to the performance Anita Dobson gave as his wife, Ange. "Anita had been around for twelve years. She'd done quite a lot of stuff before, and I think she just walked in and grabbed it. The powers-that-be liked it and the writers liked what she did with it. And because of her I became a household name." But he knew right from the outset that his past might reappear to worry him, and owned up to it before his contract for the part had been signed.

"I went to Julia and said, 'Look, before I sign the contract, there's this problem . . . and if you want to recast, fine, I understand. I don't want to jeopardise anything.' And she said, 'No, no, no, as far as I'm concerned you've got the job on merit and we'll just take it as it comes.'"

He had expected the BBC to drop him but they didn't. He repaid them well for their commitment. On the night 'Dirty Den' confessed to being the father of Michele's illegitimate baby, the audience for the programme went up by three million.

Now he's left that everyday world behind. For the moment, he's happy playing similar roles to the one which made him famous – but his sights are set on different things: "I could play the homosexual vicar. That will come later. That will come once I have financial security for my wife, my children and myself and when I am in that position I will pick what I want to do." Meanwhile he is what he is. After all, "no one accused Humphrey Bogart of being Humphrey Bogart in every part".

He thought that on a desert island he'd probably revert to childhood. His luxury was a metal detector – "so that I could imagine I was stuck on this desert island that Blackbeard had pulled in to and buried treasure. I could fill my days up just going around listening for treasure." His book, too, smacked of romantic escapism. It was *Robinson Crusoe*.

Leslie Grantham is proof that we should be careful of the judgement we make of others. He once did a terrible thing. He knows that and knows, too, that by acknowledging it he cannot exonerate himself. But by facing it, he has given himself the confidence and sense of purpose to build anew.

Leslie Grantham

Limelight (theme music from the film)
Rose Marie – Slim Whitman
Danny Boy – Jackie Wilson
The Test Pilot (sketch from 'Hancock's Half Hour')
Heartbeat – Buddy Holly
Love Walked In – Kenny Baker and Andrea Leeds
Object of My Affection – Pinky Tomlin
Every Time We Say Goodbye – Simply Red

Book: *Robinson Crusoe* (Daniel Defoe)

Luxury: *A metal detector*

SIR STEPHEN SPENDER

I'm not sure that radio does full justice to a man like Sir Stephen Spender. He carries both age and learning with great elegance. My conventional mind had led me to expect a dishevelled, battered sort of person and I felt rather ashamed when I realised that that image is just the way in which we tend to caricature our men of letters. Anyway, Stephen Spender isn't like that at all. Nor is he an old man to meet. He had come to do a good programme and to give of himself – and the result was a fascinating account of a life of great importance to English literature in the past sixty years.

Like all writers, he used my questions well. He's the sort of person who makes you feel like a good interviewer, but it's only when I'd finished and heard the recording played back that I realised that the strength of the interview lies in the skill of the answers rather than the cleverness of the questions. He had thought hard about what he wanted to say and about his records, his book and his luxury. The result was that his choices fitted easily with the various chapters of his life, giving the whole programme a clarity and coherence which made it very satisfying.

Sir Stephen Spender agreed to be photographed for this book in the London Library. Looking at his picture I find it hard to believe, as I found it hard to believe on the day we met, that the distinguished gentleman who is looking at me so charmingly, a married man for fifty years, with two grown-up children, should have been part of the avant-garde, homosexual set which so disturbed people before the last war. Inevitably it was to be the theme which dominated our conversation. He talked about it all easily and naturally. His long and full life has found room for many things which the strength of age has bound together so that none of them seems out of place.

"I feel that I am something dropped from outer space, coded with messages from all the people I know who are dead."

Sir Stephen Spender's friends are dead, but his memory keeps them alive. "I feel that I'm something dropped from outer space," he said as we began the programme, "coded with messages from all the people I know who are dead." He is constantly asked to remember stories about them, but when he does is accused of dropping names. It struck me that he was rather like a medium, and he didn't disagree. "I *feel* like a medium," he said. "One thinks of a funny story – 'Oh, I must just ring Auden and tell him that' – and then you suddenly realise Auden's dead – that's rather distressing." Now eighty years of age and far from decrepit, Stephen Spender is sustained by his long memory which, he says, has always made him feel as if he's the same person living at the same time. I wondered how old that person was. "I should think I'm what's called the permanent adolescent," he remarked. So does that mean he's just playing at being old? "Yes" – and then a pause – "or it's playing me."

Inevitably our conversation was as much about other people as it was about Stephen Spender himself. From his time as a student at Oxford in the twenties to the present day, he has known a large collection of brilliant and beautiful people. They have filled his worlds and his thoughts: they are part of him.

He became a poet in a rather conventional way. During the First World War he and his family were evacuated from the North Norfolk coast, where they lived, to Derwentwater in the Lake District to avoid the Zeppelins which tended to shed their bombs over East Anglia. Here he overheard his parents reading Wordsworth to each other. This gave him the idea of poetry "which I associated with a whole landscape". It seemed a very English reaction to his surroundings – and very poetic. He agreed. "I think of England as a very rare thing – very rare countryside, very rare people too. But when they're at their most rare I think of them as poetic. And I think I'll always remember the most beautiful poetry in the world is really English poetry."

That said, the English themselves don't always recognise this side to their nature. He had to admit that they do rather despise poetry. "One doesn't go round saying one is a poet. One doesn't write 'poet' in one's passport." What does one write? "Journalist, I think." It seemed a pity that such high-flown appreciation of his countrymen should be humbled by their lack of it.

Naturally, he could remember when he wrote his first poem. He was eight or nine, he told me, and had the courage and good humour to quote a little of it:

Oh nature, oh nature, with all thy powers
What does thou do in the long winter hours?
I love thee oh nature, so sweet and so good –
But where dost thou get thy winter food?

Not bad, I thought, for a nine-year-old – and you could spot the Wordsworth influence too. But the parents who had led him, albeit unwittingly, towards poetry died when Spender was still young, his mother when he was eleven, his father when he was sixteen. He confesses that the awful thing about their deaths was not that they were upsetting, but liberating. Following the death of his mother, he was brought home from a horrible preparatory school to be with his father. His father's death, in turn, freed him from an influence which, as an adolescent, he had come to despise. "He was a journalist in a sense which I don't really like very much," he explained, "always talking about great causes, high ideals and so on. You never felt that he was very much in touch with reality." Now, of course, he regrets the ease with which he allowed his father to leave his life. "One thing I do spend the end of my life doing is trying to mourn my father – really trying to appreciate what he was like and thinking how uncharitable for most of my life my thoughts about him have been."

It was in this "uncharitable" state of mind that the young Spender set off for Oxford – "a very affected kind of aesthete" – full of modern ideas and excited about books such as James Joyce's *Ulysses*, the literary sensation of the time. But out of some kind of masochism he rejected English and read subjects which didn't interest him at all and of which he was largely ignorant – philosophy, politics and economics. As a result, he didn't get a degree.

The other experience he enjoyed at Oxford was his friendship with W. H. Auden. Spender was two years younger than Auden and didn't get to meet him until he was in his second year. "After that we got on very well. I was already very much in the position of a disciple. He told me what poets I should like and what poetry was about." It is perhaps difficult to imagine at this distance, when we live in a much more informal age, the Oxford of the twenties. Stephen Spender had to wait to be introduced to Auden because they were at different colleges. And once they got to know each other, Spender seemed happy to slip into an admirer's role. It appeared rather different from life at a modern university. Why, I wondered, had Auden inspired such awe?

"I think he knew a very great deal. The poetry that he wrote when he was a young man is extremely beautiful, and it's also extremely difficult. His contemporaries didn't understand it very well but they did realise there was something about it which was absolutely wonderful. And then

71

he was completely sure of himself – I've never known anyone in my life who was so completely sure of himself, as Auden was."

Auden's self-assurance, Spender admitted, allowed him to be very open about his homosexuality. "We were a generation whose life-style was definitely much lower than a previous generation of Evelyn Waugh and Harold Acton. They were rather smart and moneyed. Auden, Day-Lewis, MacNeice and myself were all children of professional people – and we definitely represented a sort of lowering of social standards." Proof of this was Auden himself who, right up until the day he died, was very careless about his surroundings. "To go into a room inhabited by Auden," he told me, "was like going into the nest of some extremely untidy animal." But if they were untidy and dirty, those days were beautiful too. They still mean a great deal to Stephen Spender who, sixty and more years later, could tell me wistfully: "Those were the days. They were wonderful really. They were very free."

In the midst of all this freedom, Stephen Spender cut an eye-catching figure – "I was very tall and thin, red-faced with large blue eyes." And then, with the casual drop of another eminent name, he went on, "There's a rather famous description of me by Christopher Isherwood – 'a sort of scarlet awkward boy who thinks he's completely crazy'. And I acted rather crazy. I thought it was rather smart to be crazy: I used to read a great deal of Dostoevsky and I tried to identify myself with a character liks Aliosha in *The Brothers Karamazov*."

Next we talked about his journey to Berlin with Auden, where they first met Christopher Isherwood, and where for a while they lived. Their move there was, he explained, a reaction against the Bloomsbury set's love of Paris – "smart and sophisticated," he remembered, "and they were always talking about it in their rather fluty voices. Berlin was rough – and, incidentally, not a bit like the city portrayed in the film *Cabaret*.

"I remarked to Isherwood when I'd seen *Cabaret* that there wasn't anything in it that we could have afforded to do when we were living in Berlin nor could Sally Bowles, whom I knew very well. If you associate us with Berlin you mustn't think of that transvestite kind of very decadent Berlin. You must think of something rougher – sort of working-class young men and boys who were unemployed and were very glad to have friends like us. It was much more like that."

It was the early thirties and Spender witnessed in Berlin the beginnings of Nazism. His feelings were very much to the left, but he asked himself whether he was being stupid in not giving Nazi ideas fair play in his thinking. On reading Nazi literature he discovered with relief that his first impressions had been correct.

"I thought they were not only wicked but they were extremely cynical.

I think it was Hitler or Goebbels who said, 'If you want the people to believe a lie, tell the biggest lie possible.' A man who was supposed to be a leader of the people was boasting of the fact that he had told his followers the biggest lies possible and they were all delighted. Nazism was like being given a bottle of medicine which has 'poison' written very large on the label and the person who gets the bottle is delighted to drink it. It was an extremely cynical movement."

Notwithstanding that his trip to Berlin was prompted by his distaste for Bloomsbury attitudes, Spender eventually fell under the spell of that literary set. Recognition by the great is bound to have both pitfalls and compensations. He was more than twenty years younger than T. S. Eliot and Virginia Woolf, who were both "extremely nice" to him. "Of course one knows what Virginia really thought of one because she wrote her journals, all of which have been published. Some remarks about me are extremely snide – but there are also some very nice remarks too. Within limits I had a very real understanding with her. She was always supposed to be very touchy and to snub people. I think I was aware – perhaps because of my mother who was also a bit mad – I was aware of this extreme sensitivity."

One of Stephen Spender's funniest recollections of his Bloomsbury days is his account of tea at Lady Ottoline Morrell's. "She was a great hostess. She was somewhat grotesque, if one can say this politely, and dressed almost like an eighteenth-century shepherdess. She was extremely open in her conversation and really adored intellectuals – Bertrand Russell, with whom she had a love affair, Aldous Huxley and D. H. Lawrence, with whom I strongly suspect she had a love affair.

"Once she invited me to tea alone. It began with her dropping her earring into the teacup and the next thing was, the whole front of her dress had come down and there were her naked breasts. I sort of had to wait, embarrassed, while she tucked them up. She was extremely eccentric, I must say."

The war, which changed everything, changed Stephen Spender too. With Berlin and Bloomsbury behind him, he fell in love – "it just happened" – and in 1942 married the pianist Natasha Litvin with whom he has spent his life ever since. Apart from seven years at London University, he has earned most of his money teaching in America where, by then an established family man, he kept in touch with Auden and Isherwood. Their friendship, however, had clouded. Auden and Isherwood seemed annoyed, says Spender, that he had moved away from homosexuality and fallen in love with a woman.

"I didn't quite understand how annoyed they were. I think that homosexuality is very cliquey – it was particularly then – and one had betrayed the side – a side which is sort of persecuted. In Isherwood's case he could almost identify the persecution of homosexuals with the persecution of the Jews, an attitude I disagreed with. But if he had that attitude then he would deplore the abandonment, as he'd think of it, of the tribe or the cause by any of its members."

Stephen Spender doesn't worry about death. He doesn't want to have a long illness, "which would be a great nuisance to everyone" – so he hopes he'll just "drop dead". As we talked about the end of his life, I thought back to its beginning, to the impressionable young man who, relieved of his parents' influence, had gone to Oxford, swaggered with the outlandish and the fashionable, and then settled down to a life in which he had been honoured as an Englishman of letters. Researching the programme, I had discovered that Cyril Connolly had said of him that he was two people – one an inspired simpleton, the other a ruthless and ambitious intellectual. Did he recognise either description?

"I recognise the descriptions, of course. He thought I was ruthless because anyone who worked seriously, he thought of as being ruthless and trying to steal an advantage over him."

And the simpleton?

"I think it's rather flattering, as a matter of fact. I would replace it with simple-*minded* or *single*-minded – but again it goes back to the Dostoyevskian idea of the holy fool, the Aliosha, and I wish I was that or had been that."

As his luxuries, Stephen Spender chose Proust to read and a painting or sculpture by his son, Matthew, with a photograph of his daughter, Lizzie, stuck on the back. Possessed of a good book and these simple mementoes, he was ready to begin his exile on the desert island. The comfort of his old age, however, seemed to belie the turbulence of his youth. In talking to him, I felt his early years had chased his later ones until, exhausted by the effort of pursuit, they had let slip their hold. I didn't recognise Cyril Connolly's contrast between inspired simpleton and ambitious intellectual. But I still saw two men – one young, careless and free, the other old, wiser and contained.

Sir Stephen Spender

Act 2 of *Falstaff* (Verdi)
String Quartet No. 15 in A minor (Beethoven)
Act 1 of *The Rake's Progress* (Stravinsky)
I'm a Tree – Douglas Byng
Allegretto from Piano sonata No. 20 in A, D959 (Schubert)
Piano Concerto No. 2 in B flat (Beethoven) – Natasha Litvin
(the castaway's wife)
String Quartet in F minor Op. 20 No. 5 (Haydn)
Act 3 of *Twilight of the Gods* (Wagner)

Book: *Remembrance of Things Past* (Marcel Proust)

Luxury: *A painting or sculpture by his son, Matthew, with a photograph of his daughter, Lizzie, stuck on the back*

ARTHUR SCARGILL

I first met Arthur Scargill at a Labour Party Conference in Blackpool in the mid-seventies. I was working for *Nationwide* which was then the BBC's early evening television current affairs programme. We had a camera position on the balcony overlooking the body of the hall. Here we would quickly record interviews and send them down the line to London for inclusion in that night's edition. Arthur Scargill had just finished a rousing speech. It had not pleased all the Labour Party hierarchy, but it had thrilled the delegates. He had been received with delighted applause.

The session over, he and his senior colleagues in the National Union of Mineworkers made their way out of the hall, receiving congratulations as they did so. I knew we wanted to interview him, and was frightened we would miss the opportunity. Without a second thought I leaned over the balcony and shouted: "Arthur! Arthur Scargill! Look up here!" He looked. So did everyone else.

"Mr Scargill!" I continued, "we want to interview you for *Nationwide*. Could you come up here now?" And then, aware that my entreaties were somewhat conspicuous, added: "Oh dear. I feel a bit like Juliet stuck up here."

"In that case," shouted back Mr Scargill, his face just one of many which were now peering upwards, "I shall be Romeo. I'll come and do the interview now."

It was as good an introduction as any. I can't say that after that we always met on such friendly terms. I remember many viewers rallied to his defence when they felt I had been rude to him during an interview about the miners' strike on the *Six O'Clock News*. I hadn't intended to be – and I think Arthur Scargill knew that because, when I rang him to invite him on *Desert Island Discs*, I was put straight through to his office without any of the filtering process that usually surrounds him.

He was my third guest on the programme and, as it turned out, the one with whom we recorded more material than anyone else. (That record still stands.) But the even-handed logic of the radio schedule cut him like all the others. The final programme was no different in shape or length from the rest.

Arthur Scargill is a man whom many people might like to see on a desert island. He is extremely popular with the men he leads and often intensely disliked by those with whom he clashes. But about one thing there can be no argument: as President of the NUM he has defended his causes with a passion which makes him impossible to ignore.

"What I did was right – and above all, I never sold out the men."

The image which many people have of him does not worry Arthur Scargill at all. It was the first thing I said to him. "Like it or not, you are something of a *bête noire* to many."

"It doesn't worry me," he replied calmly. "It sometimes saddens me that people can have an image of a person that's not true – and I suspect it's comparable with the soap operas on television. I think what happens is that the image of Arthur Scargill disguises the reality of the person. It's only when people actually meet me that they discover the real me. When they do, by and large they say, You are different from the person we thought you were."

It was a typical response from a man who seemed very self-confident and at ease with himself. He knew exactly what he thought, and precisely what he wanted to say.

Arthur Scargill revealed that ever since he had received my invitation he had been thinking about how he would cope on the desert island. "I'm a dab hand at making fish and chips, and I would certainly have a go at constructing a hut of some kind." He said he was orderly in his everyday life and that he would try and get some kind of a plan together. It would enable him to have a store of food and proper living accommodation, "so that until the time came when I was rescued, hopefully, I would survive in surroundings that were at least reasonable".

His first record turned out to be 'The Entertainer' by Scott Joplin – an appropriate piece of music for a man who enjoys performing in front of an audience. He admitted there was something of the entertainer in him – particularly when he's making a speech. "I think you see a completely different Arthur Scargill in those circumstances than you do, for instance, on television or on a radio programme. The fact is that you're able to give the complete picture in, say, a forty- or fifty-minute speech, and you're able to throw pieces of humour into it. You are not able to do that when you are being very severely cross-examined by a television or a radio interviewer."

He denied that he enjoyed the sense of power which his oratory gives him. It is commitment, not glamour, which drives him. "I believe in what I'm doing. I find that because I believe so passionately in what I do, it communicates itself to the audience. That's the reason you can feel them going with you, coming to their feet at certain points and clapping you very loudly. I suspect that anybody who has been in that position will confirm this view. If you speak very passionately about something that matters, your audience begins to identify with you."

As a small boy attending the local primary and secondary schools in

Worborough Dale in Yorkshire, Arthur was "a bit of a rebel". He was not, he said, the sort of child others naturally followed. He was never chosen as a captain, a monitor or a prefect. But he was "reasonably popular". He played soccer, was pretty good at wrestling and for ten years did judo. "It's all come in useful," he said, "particularly in certain instances when kiosk doors have been wrenched open and blokes with snooker cues have appeared" – a reference to a notorious incident when he and a political opponent tangled in a public telephone box.

Scargill was an only child and very close to his mother. She had been told, after producing a stillborn child, that she would not be able to have children. When she was thirty-two, she discovered she was pregnant with Arthur. Her death, when he was eighteen, affected him deeply.

"I remember my mother with probably more vivid recollection than anything else my in life. When she died – for three months, it literally rendered me unable to function properly. I was very, very close to my mother. In the Second World War my father was in the Royal Air Force, and so my mother and I became inseparable. She died when she was fifty years of age. She was a Christian. She was a lovely woman, and obviously I loved her very much indeed. I often think back and regret deeply that she never saw any of the things that I was able to achieve in later life. The only things that she ever saw me do were to go down the pit, and join the Young Communist League. Both of those things she disapproved of, because she didn't want me to get hurt down the pit, and she didn't want me to get hurt by joining the Young Communist League." I wondered if she would have been proud of his achievements today: "I'm sure my mother would have been as proud of me as I was of her," he replied calmly.

Arthur Scargill's father was a miner and a Communist, the very opposite of his mother who was a Christian. "My mother was strictly non-political. My father was very political indeed, and I was brought up in a household filled with love, but also filled with this marvellous contradiction: my mother who used to go to church, and my father who used to go to the Communist Party meeting, and to the meetings of the National Union of Mineworkers."

Opposite points of view, however, did not make for an argumentative household. "My mother totally supported my father, absolutely loved him, and of course it was reciprocated. But I found that I used to have lots of discussions with my father, although he never, ever tried to persuade me to adopt his political persuasion. He thought it was best that I make up my own mind, and it wasn't until I was about fourteen that I asked him if I could go to a political meeting with him."

Arthur left school at fifteen. He wanted to get a job in engineering but failed to find one. So, like many lads in the same situation, he followed his father down the pit. "The first day at work was almost indescribable.

I remember walking to the pit yard at Woolley, which is a colliery to the north of Barnsley, and it was a dank, dark morning, and I was put into the engineering office to wait the big man coming along. There were about six of us waiting. And he duly came into the office at about ten minutes to six, and he was wearing a pork pie hat, and he says, 'Well, what have we got here?' And what we'd got here, of course, was six young lads who were terrified. And he told his assistant to take us down into the screens. A screening plant was an area where you had a job picking out the rock from the coal as it went past on a conveyer belt, and we went across the pit yard, and down some steps, under some very dark areas, and then down some more steps into an area which I can only describe as being comparable to Dante's Inferno. The dust was so thick you couldn't see more than about a foot or two foot in front of you. And the noise was so intense that I actually learned within the space of three weeks to speak with sign language. I had to exist in that atmosphere for nearly a year, and it certainly had a tremendous influence on the way that I reacted towards other people."

It was obviously a scene which he had described before. Its awfulness was exciting and challenging. Mining may send men into a noisy hell, but it retains a romantic image. Arthur Scargill acknowledges this. "If it's not being sexist," he said, "I suppose it's like being married. You have amazing rows but you always go back. I think what it is, is that there is a degree of comradeship in the mining industry that you'll not find anywhere else, apart, probably, from the fishing industry. And it's because of the closeness of the people in the environment in which they work. I recall vividly, working with these young lads in really dangerous circumstances, and feeling a sympathy for them and them for me, so that if one of them was threatened with anything, disciplined by the management, for instance, we saw it as an attack upon ourselves."

Men who are attacked need someone to defend them, and Arthur Scargill quickly assumed that rôle. Very early in his mining career he took up the cause of a group of young men with whom he was working. He discovered that on the day before a public holiday, unlike everybody else in the pit, the youngsters were not allowed to go home as soon as they had finished their work. They asked Arthur to speak up for them.

"I went into the manager's office. It seemed to me that it was about three hundred feet in length, it took so long to walk across the room. The manager was sitting there smoking a pipe, and he said, 'What's thou want, lad?' And I said, 'Well, I've come to represent all the lads in the pit bottom.' 'Oh aye, about what?' And so I explained the case to him, and I said, 'And what we're asking, Mr Steele, is for permission for us to go home when we've completed our work, just today.' He said, 'Thou knows I can't give you that permission', and just as we were going to the door he said, 'Thou'd be better off training in Moscow there, rather than here', and I went out. And I thought, I haven't succeeded in those negotiations. But I suddenly realised he hadn't said 'No'. He'd simply said he couldn't give us permission. And so when the time came at the end of the shift for us to come out, I promptly led them all out with the rest of the men, and to everybody's astonishment, we all got paid our full wages, and from that moment on, I was regarded as something of a champion in the pit."

In his mid-twenties, Scargill had the opportunity to go to university: not as a student, but as a miner attending on a day release arrangement. "The National Union of Mineworkers had adopted a scheme for sending what it called its 'talented young people' to university on a day release course for three years, and we could go along and take economics, industrial relations, and social history. You could either go to the University of Leeds or the University of Sheffield, dependent of course on being accepted. I went to the University of Leeds for three years. I actually got offered a place at Oxford as a result of that but couldn't afford to go. But during the time that I was at the university, I learned many skills including one which I've always been very, very pleased that I adopted – the ability to read newspapers very quickly indeed. Ironically, the tutor at Leeds University was a former aide to Winston Churchill, and he was the man who taught me how to do this reading of a newspaper very quickly."

By this stage we'd come to the moment for Arthur Scargill to choose his fifth record. In doing so he revealed a sentimental side to his character. He'd already told me about his Airedale dogs and his geese called – "appropriately enough" – Gaddafi, Gorbachev and Gromyko. Now he wanted a piece of music to remind him of his love for his dogs – and chose 'Old Shep' sung by Elvis Presley. The interlude over, we continued further down the main road of his life. Had he, I asked him, ever been tempted to go in for politics proper and try for a seat at Westminster?

"Quite the reverse. I was actually tempted in my younger days, when I was fifteen or sixteen, to try for a full-blooded political career, which would involve standing for the local council, which I did, and eventually hopefully standing for Parliament. But then I made a quite conscious decision to concentrate my work in the trade union movement. I've been offered at least six parliamentary seats during the past fourteen or fifteen years – and I mean that quite seriously. They were all offers of safe seats. None of them was I tempted to take. I've also been offered, of course, leading positions in the National Coal Board, and I wasn't tempted to take those either."

More recently, of course, Arthur Scargill has talked about becoming an MP. But our conversation took place in early 1988 when he was extremely dismissive about the strength of a seat in Parliament. "In real terms, power is in the trade union and Labour movement. Unless you are a Cabinet Minister, you're really not in a situation or a position where you are going to be able to achieve anything. And if you look at the average span, when a person is in a Cabinet, it's very limited indeed. An ordinary MP can't get very much done. That's not to criticise them, because they do as well as they are able in the circumstances that present themselves."

As far as Arthur Scargill is concerned, MPs are anonymous whereas trade union leaders are familiar figures. Ask the public for the names of MPs and they won't know. "On the other hand, if you ask them who is President of the NUM, or who is the General Secretary of the Transport and General Workers Union, I've no doubt they'd tell you instantly."

It was a confident affirmation of the power and rôle of the trade unions. So did he believe that by the end of this century his kind of socialist Britain would be in place? "I'm not a dreamer, but what I am is a believer in the socialist system. The one thing I would never do is to be daft enough to commit myself to say it will occur on such-and-such a date, or at such-and-such a time. Because I know from experience, not only here, but in many parts of the world, that circumstances can alter quite dramatically, and change things literally overnight. So all I would say is that the inevitability of socialism is there for all to see. We can't carry on with a system where we produce too much food, and put it into great big warehouses to rot, at the same time as we see people die of starvation in the Third World. If for no other reason than wanting to bring about a world without nuclear weapons, a world of peace, I think Britain and its people will eventually turn towards a socialist alternative."

Arthur Scargill's convictions had, more than those of anyone else, led the miners into their year-long strike in 1984. It was, I reminded him, often called 'Scargill's Strike'. Surely here was something upon which to reflect while he was cast away on his desert island. Alone and away from it all would he ever say to himself: "I should have done that differently"?

His answer was uncompromising: "I don't think I would do anything differently, quite frankly. And that's not to be bigoted. The strike was created deliberately by both the National Coal Board and the Conservative government's intention to bring about a pit closure programme. Tragically, not only were there many people outside the mining industry who didn't believe me, including the media; there were also sections of the Miners' Union who didn't believe me either. They thought I was scaremongering. They thought that I was just merely flying a kite. I think that the events over the past three or four years have demonstrated that I was absolutely correct." Arthur Scargill not only maintains that he was right. He also argues that he didn't lose.

"I don't accept that in the end we lost. I think that if you look at the strike itself and take it into context, you'll see that it led to an inspiration as far as the Labour and trade union movement is concerned. It's often been said in history that people have lost things. It was said the suffragettes lost, but as you and I talk here today you know that the suffragettes didn't lose. It was said that the Tolpuddle Martyrs lost, but when you look back, we know that the trade union movement in this country, and in other parts of the world, flourished because of their sacrifice. I think that eventually we shall see not only the triumph of working people in establishing the right to work, but we shall see the establishment of socialism *because of*, and not *in spite of*, the miners' strike."

I asked him then about the personal aspects of the strike. With his reputation for being a workaholic, I wondered how he had coped with very little sleep and constant pressure. Had he ever cracked — even for a brief moment? Once again, his answer was implacable.

"Never once. And the reason's a simple one. I believed passionately in what I was doing, and I knew that the cause was absolutely right. When I'm sitting on that desert island, I'll be able to sit back, under the palm tree, looking out over that beautiful stretch of sand, and say to myself, 'What I did was right, and above all, I never sold out the men'."

But for his family, too, there must have been pressures. Did they ever wish they didn't carry the Scargill name? Smiling, he admitted that sometimes life could be difficult.

"My wife went to the dentist in the middle of the miners' strike, and he looked at the card, and said, 'Scargill?' And she said, 'Yeah', because she had her mouth spragged open with these pincers. And he said, 'Any relation to the miners' leader?' And she shook her head and said, 'No. None whatsoever.' Which I think was prudent on her part at the time."

He laughed as he told this story and it made me laugh too. Gradually we were drawing away from the serious centre to Arthur Scargill's life. However much he may believe in what he does and what he stands for, he is still quite capable of laughing at himself. "I wouldn't be sitting down doing nothing on the desert island, you know. I'd be making my plans so that you would have the benefit of my immoderate approach back here in Britain."

A good answer; and once again it revealed a complete lack of self-doubt. Was that a strength — or a weakness? How would he answer those who said he couldn't take criticism, that he was too single-minded?

"I would say that's a matter for them to determine and not for me. But if the criticism is that I'm single-minded, I plead guilty. If the criticism is that I don't doubt what I'm doing is right, I plead guilty. And I think it's important that that's understood, because I *can* accept criticism, and obviously I discuss things with my colleagues. I think it's important, in trade unionism, that people understand that they've got someone who is prepared to lead from the front."

Leading from the front. It could be Arthur Scargill's epitaph. He had been robust and frank in his conversation with me and, I thought, revealed a lot about who he is and how he thinks. But there was one more revelation to come. I think, of all the castaways I have interviewed on *Desert Island Discs*, the luxury chosen by Arthur Scargill was the most surprising and interesting.

"I'd like," he said, "a little-known painting called the *Mona Lisa*. Could I have it?"

Of course he could. *Desert Island Discs* promises you everything, as long as you're playing the game. But why? He revealed that at one time, although he had never seen it, he regarded the painting as overrated. Then, during a period when he was making frequent visits to France, he decided to go and look at it – for no other reason than to say that he had done so.

"I went and looked at the painting, and I suddenly realised what da Vinci had done. He had painted a masterpiece. Probably the greatest painting of all time. I fell in love with it then, and I'm still in love with it now."

The picture of Arthur Scargill alone on a desert island with the *Mona Lisa* nailed to a palm tree as he laid his plans for the socialist future of Britain seemed an appropriate one with which to end the programme. He would draw comfort, I thought, from that unblinking smile. Not even she could tell him when he might be wrong.

Arthur Scargill

The Entertainer (Scott Joplin)
Oh Love That Will Not Let Me Go (hymn)
Overture to *Orpheus in the Underworld* (Offenbach)
Beale Street Blues – Louis Armstrong and His All Stars
Old Shep – Elvis Presley
1812 Overture (Tchaikovsky) – Massed Brass Bands of Yorkshire
No Regrets – Edith Piaf
Chorus of the Hebrew Slaves from *Nabucco* (Verdi)

Book: *Huckleberry Finn* (Mark Twain)

Luxury: *The Mona Lisa*

SIR CLAUS MOSER

Desert Island Discs might have been created with Sir Claus Moser in mind. He loves music, he has done several very interesting jobs and he has had a dramatic personal life. From the outset he was very clear about what he wanted to say and how he thought the programme should be structured. He knew instinctively that it was ideal for someone of his abilities and taste and he was anxious that the moment should not be lost.

For me, of course, there's a certain disadvantage in dealing with someone who is fully prepared. It gives me very little room for manoeuvre. My opportunities to shape the programme are automatically reduced. So to begin with, I think there was a certain amount of creative tension during our recording. Sir Claus Moser would ask that things be done one way. I would suggest another.

If anyone wants proof that creative tension is a force for good, they should listen to this recording again. I think it turned out to be one of the most interesting programmes we made, the result of careful discussion and, in the end, mutual respect. His concern to get it right fuelled my anxiety to deliver something that he felt was a fair reflection of his life and together we made a programme that was satisfyingly complete.

If you had told me during the first part of the recording, as we struggled and juggled with our material, that Sir Claus Moser and I would strike up a friendship, I would have told you that such an occurrence was most unlikely. But we have, proving once again that *Desert Island Discs* is a duet, not a solo performance.

". . . deep down I still regard myself as not totally
English . . . I am a European. Above all, I'm a Jew."

Sir Claus Moser's profession is statistics, but his love is music. It has been a dominating force since his childhood in Berlin. Now, as the Warden of an Oxford college, he can look back on a life whose variety has enjoyed music as one of its main unifying themes. His appreciation of it started early. "The great evenings of the Berlin days were evenings when my parents had rather superior musicians come to play *with* them. My mother would play with great musicians. I was meant to be in bed, but I crouched under the staircase listening. I just loved it – and I've loved it ever since. I've loved playing and I've loved listening." His parents were well off. His father was a banker and the family had a lovely home. Young Claus was taken to lots of concerts, but never allowed to stay until the end. Come the interval, he was sent home to bed. It was both instructive and disappointing at the same time: "I always wanted more. And I didn't discover how *Aida* ended until quite late in life."

For the Mosers, as for many families in the Germany of the 1930s, the shadow of Nazism fell across them. "It was a happy home and music was part of the happiness, but the other part, which really has been basic to my whole life, was the happiness of the family. My parents, my brother and I were always very close – and we had, of course, a wider family."

No wonder, then, that he can remember very clearly the moment when his contentment came under threat. It was 30 January 1933. Hitler had come to power, and the torchlight processions had begun.

"I was eleven. I can see myself standing at the window and watching it. But I can't honestly pretend that the years when we remained in Germany, from 1933 to 1936, were miserable years for me. I can't say that.

"There were roughly thirty boys in my class and two of us were Jews. And the teacher came in every morning and said 'Heil Hitler' and the boys stood up and said 'Heil Hitler' with the Hitler sign. The two Jewish boys, me and the other one, were not allowed to stand. Of course we didn't want to stand up and say 'Heil Hitler' – but it was a daily humiliation. Then one had fights in the breaks between lessons."

Increasingly he came to understand what was going on around him. "I saw Hitler dozens of times parading up and down – and Goebbels and Goering. My father had decided as long ago as 1929 that there was no future for us Jews in Germany and he decided then that we would emigrate. The only reason we didn't go until 1936 was because my grandmother was too old to move. So it was part of family conversation. We understood that we were in the firing line. What we couldn't have understood at that time was that it was going to lead, from 1938 onwards, to six million deaths. We couldn't have understood then what lay ahead. After all, in 1936 when we came out we still managed to come out freely. Not with everything, but with something."

At this juncture of our conversation we paused. For his second record, Claus Moser chose Louis Kentner playing Liszt's 'Bénédiction de Dieu dans la solitude'. In the twenties, in a childhood still unhampered by Europe's impending catastrophe, Claus Moser was taught the piano by a woman who claimed to have been a pupil of Liszt. Her claim could never be proved – but her ability as a teacher persuaded the young boy that he, too, wanted to be a pianist when he grew up. That never happened. But sixty years later, the great Kentner took the musical Moser as his pupil for five years. It was, says Moser, "the climax of my musical life. He so loved playing the piano that he inspired one to share that love – a great, wonderful man and musician."

Our interlude over, we moved back into the mainstream of Claus Moser's life. In 1936 he and his family left Berlin, bound originally for America – "but we stayed here in Britain happily". Once again, however, happiness was interrupted. In May 1940 he was interned.

"My father, my brother and I were taken to Lingfield Racecourse – the first time I've ever slept in a racecourse – and there we were for two or three days. It was rather miserable – but it's very important to put this in perspective. It was miserable for the older generation. My brother and I were very young. I was actually under-age, which was why I was released fairly quickly – after only three months. But for the older generation it was humiliating. After all, my father and mother had given up a great deal. He was at the peak of his career, fifty-one when he left Germany."

There were, he remembers, some suicides in the camp. People couldn't quite understand why they were there.

"It was a real puzzle. We certainly understood that the British government were very worried about spies, but I think it was quite hard to take that, in order to catch a few spies, all the enemy aliens, as we were called, had to be put behind bars. Why did we have to be stripped of all our valuables when we came in?"

But there were lighter moments too. He recalls that in Highton Internment Camp, in the middle of the Battle of Britain in June 1940, there would miraculously appear a Viennese café – with cream cakes, iced coffee and all the other trappings. He has no idea where it came from. "I remember that the army officers who were our guards used to share these enjoyments with us. There was a bank. I've often wondered about this since, because there was nothing to buy. But you know, if you put 5,000 Jews behind barbed wire we all find something to do."

Eventually the war effort found something for Claus Moser to do.

Released from internment, he applied to join the RAF. They told him he could become a flight mechanic. He was thrilled, assuming that he was going to be able to put into practice his mathematics and statistics. He didn't realise that flight mechanics were otherwise known as 'grease monkeys' whose basic job was to keep aeroplanes clean and running smoothly. He now regards this time in his life as very important. "I loved it. I look back on those three years as very important, not because we won the war but because I realised what a prig I was – I really was. I'd had a very glossy youth and life and I hadn't really mixed with a wide range of people. In the RAF I did. I learned a lot from that."

I thought this an interesting piece of self-awareness. The life of cultured ease he had described at the beginning of the programme had been so beguiling that I hadn't seen the other side of it. Only when he admitted to his priggishness did I realise that a young man brought up in such a world could easily become aloof and superior. I could also begin to see how Claus Moser had become a successful man. Intelligence taught him to treat every change of circumstances as an opportunity. Whether he was a comfortable intellectual youth in Berlin, an exile, or a grease monkey in the wartime RAF, he seemed able to turn his immediate environment to his future advantage.

After the war he moved to the London School of Economics as a lecturer and began to write books on statistics – a subject which, I reminded him, he himself had described as "boringly, germanically systematic".

"I'd forgotten that description. It's very accurate. One of them is a textbook which still sells, I'm happy to say. I did meet a former student of mine the other day who said it was the most boring book she'd ever read."

It struck me as odd that a man of such sensitivity should draw so much enjoyment from the dry world of statistics. Sir Claus took exception to my description of his subject.

"I don't regard it as dry," he replied. "I believe that statistics, good statistics – just like good writing – have a tremendously compassionate job to do in throwing light on the life of people. All my statistical work, both when I was writing books and when I was Head of Government Statistics, related to that."

His passion for his work earned him a suitable reward. In 1967 the Prime Minister, Harold Wilson, asked Claus Moser to become Director of the Central Statistical Office.

"What rather amused me about my appointment was that four years earlier I had applied to the Central Statistical Office to work there as an ordinary statistician. I was told 'no' in view of my German birth. As it was a high-security office in Whitehall, the Cabinet Office, this was not on. When Prime Minister Wilson asked me to be the head of it, that little problem was suddenly overcome. I was allowed in as the head – but I hadn't been allowed in as one of the underlings."

Such are the ways of the British Establishment. Once in, Sir Claus found himself in a world that he thoroughly enjoyed. He served three Prime Ministers – Wilson, Heath and Callaghan. "It was a wonderful decade for me. It was heady stuff. I was at the centre of policy-making and as I believed passionately in the importance of statistics for democracy I worked myself very hard to try to serve the government."

Were there not times, I asked tentatively, when eminent men, Prime Ministers among them, required Moser's statistics to be 'massaged'? I used the euphemism deliberately – and he knew what I meant.

"There were a number of occasions when I had cause to be unhappy about Ministers," came the prompt reply. "But all my life I've believed in fighting for what I am doing. I don't believe in silence, so I always fought."

From his career in statistics we moved back to music, to talk about his long association with the Royal Opera House as a member of its board and, in due course, its Chairman. For Sir Claus Moser this was another high point in his life. Again it was something that he loved (how lucky, I thought, that a man should do so many things in his life which he liked so much) and the only reason why he'd decided not to take all operatic or balletic records to his desert island was to give himself a break from the two thousand performances he'd seen at Covent Garden. His many attendances were undoubtedly a mark of his devotion – but a badge of privilege too. How did he answer the accusation that the Royal Opera House was an élitist institution?

"There's image and reality. It's inevitable that a place which is a grand building will always have a bit of an image of élitism. It is also inevitable, given the financing – which I'm very unhappy about – that a lot of prices are rather high. It is also inevitable that they will get higher because the pressure of the present government is on self-help. That includes the box-office."

He accepts that some productions have been over-elaborate – "I care about the music above all." However, Covent Garden, he thinks, must still find room for highly expensive international stars. "Don't forget that the public do want to hear Domingo – they do want to hear Jessye Norman."

Sir Claus Moser has enjoyed two other careers, neither of which we found very much time to talk about during the programme. Although he had planned to stay in Whitehall until he retired, he suddenly received an invitation from Rothschild's, the bankers, to join them. So, at the age of fifty-seven, he moved into his father's profession. But, he admitted, banking was not something which was in his blood. "I don't think one *becomes* a natural banker at the age of fifty-seven." His last career – at least at the time of writing – is as Warden of Wadham College, Oxford – an elegant life, but exciting too. "The excitement is the mix of youngsters. It makes me feel quite young again. It's most satisfying working with the young."

It occurred to me that his life had come full circle. That by taking up his father's profession, enjoying the prestige of his Oxford position, and by remaining in close touch with the world of music through the Opera House, he had somehow recreated the kind of world in which his family had lived in Berlin half a century ago. It was an idea he found too romantic.

"I don't think I've gone back to the life-style where I began. But I think the elements are there – namely, respect for a profession, which is to me being an academic; respect for the private sector, which is banking; and above all the importance of education and the arts. That's what makes up this funny mishmash that I've lived."

Mishmash seems rather a clumsy word for a man as refined and intelligent as Sir Claus Moser. But his life has been a mixture of many things – not only professionally but linguistically and culturally too. Did he feel himself to be British? Or was he in his heart still German?

"Not German. I am British, as we like to say. But deep down I still regard myself as not totally English. I'm not, after all. I'm not saying anything very significant in saying that. I'm partly foreign, and I'm neither proud of it nor ashamed of it. I am a European. Above all, I'm a Jew. I don't regard myself now as a refugee; I don't regard myself as without roots; I don't regard myself as insecure. If I said any of those things it would be false. I think the fact is, though, that when I became head of a major government department – the Central Statistical Office – within a top-security office, the Cabinet Office, I was rather proud to be so appointed and part of my pride was that this happened to somebody who hadn't come up the straight, Eton-Oxford route – you know what I mean? And I must confess that when I was knighted, again that gave me an extra little bit of pleasure. Above all, I confess that when I was appointed first to the Board of Covent Garden, and then Chairman, I was absolutely astonished that, having come from a childhood where from very early days, when I was five, six or seven, music and opera were part of my life and happiness – it absolutely amazed me that Britain could appoint somebody from outside to this, dare I say it, top job in the arts."

It was an answer that shone with pride mixed with modesty. Natural talent and intelligence have placed Sir Claus Moser at the top of the society in which he lives. Because it is not the society into which he was born, he has had to work hard for his achievements. It is something which obviously gives him enormous pleasure. For him it has all been worth while. The word 'happiness' recurs throughout the descriptions of his life – from his childhood in Berlin to his life now in London and Oxford.

We came to his last record. It had to be from Mozart's *Marriage of Figaro*, he told me, not only because it is "the most perfect opera ever written" but because it had also provided him with one of the most memorable evenings in his life.

"On my retirement from the Royal Opera House, they decided to give me, as a present to my wife and myself, a performance – and when the cast bowed to me, led by Haitink at the end, I thought for a moment that perhaps Mozart had written it for me."

In the studio you could have heard a pin drop. Sir Claus Moser, statistician, banker, academic and musician, had been moved to the bottom of his heart. After that there was little more to say. He would take James Thurber with him – "I need a bit of a laugh every now and then" – and a Steinway grand.

I do not know who would hear him, on his desert island, as he attempted to recreate the sounds which the great Louis Kentner had taught him. But I do know this: they would be sounds which come from a man whose accomplishments have always prevented him from being stranded.

Sir Claus Moser

Trio in B flat Op. 97, 'Archduke' (Beethoven)
Bénédiction de Dieu dans la solitude (Liszt) – Louis Kentner
String Quintet in G minor, K516 (Mozart)
Fantasia in F minor Op. 103 (Schubert)
Double Violin Concerto (Bach)
Vespers (Monteverdi)
Wotan's Farewell from *Die Walküre* (Wagner)
Sextet from *The Marriage of Figaro* (Mozart)

Book: *A volume of James Thurber*

Luxury: *A Steinway grand piano*

HRH THE DUCHESS OF KENT

I had interviewed Her Royal Highness the Duchess of Kent once before, on television. I had thought then that she would make an ideal castaway and was glad she felt able to accept our invitation to be a Christmas guest for the programme.

She's always been one of the more accessible members of the Royal Family. In her work for charity, particularly with old people and with hospice work, she's felt able to reveal a great deal about her own feelings. At the same time she is someone who obviously enjoys laughter and the sharing with others of many of life's everyday pleasures. The experience of growing up in a big, happy Yorkshire family has never left her – and she referred to it often in our programme.

Then there is her love of music – it has played an important part in her life and her eight records were not only thoughtfully chosen but related closely to people whom she knew.

Royal interviews are different from others. They are occasions when journalism must at times defer to protocol. I think the audience understands and expects this. But they expect a good programme too, and thanks to Her Royal Highness's readiness to speak freely about her childhood, her wedding and her work, on this occasion they got it.

"My first feeling for music stemmed, I am sure, from a
musical box of my father's."

"I can think of absolutely nothing nicer than being cast away on a desert island," announced Her Royal Highness, the Duchess of Kent, at the start of the programme. The thought that she would have no timetable to keep, and would be able to live there just being herself, appealed to her very much. The romance of the idea had caught her imagination too. She could see herself swimming, fishing or shinning up a tree to keep an eye out for passing ships. It all seemed a long way away from the pressures of public display and the duties of royalty. No wonder she found it so attractive.

The idylls of radio's island were matched by the Duchess's love of music. "I get very emotional about music. I studied it until I married and was very sad to slowly have to reduce the time I devoted to it. But I am now participating in music again — as well as listening — which has given me an enormous amount of pleasure." All the music which she chose for the programme meant something to her personally, either in itself or because she knew the performers. It started with a Mozart piano sonata which she played in front of her parents in the school hall when she was twelve — she remembered that she got the first chord wrong — and went on to include performances by such distinguished friends as Placido Domingo, Georg Solti and Jacqueline du Pré.

Music attracted the Duchess of Kent from a very early age. "I remember a lovely Victorian musical box my father had, which I now have. And I remember listening with my ear on it when I was only about three. Listening, feeling the vibration of the music coming through. My first feeling for music stemmed, I am sure, from a musical box of my father's."

She was born in Yorkshire as Katharine Worsley, the only daughter of Sir William and Lady Worsley of Hovingham Hall. "It's an incredibly beautiful place. The country round is heather and rolling hills. My father had a passion for forestry, and so I lived among beautiful woods. And he would make them particularly beautiful because he would plant, along the outsides of the forests, cherries and maples, so that people driving past saw beauty as well as the not-so-beautiful hardwoods or softwoods that he was planting for commercial purposes."

Her childhood was privileged but informal. She had "lovely trusting parents" who allowed her to be something of a tomboy in the company of three older brothers. Hence her ability to shin up a tree, a pastime which she admitted is "still not unnatural to me". The Hall had a cricket pitch too. Her father captained Yorkshire before the Duchess was born but she met many people with whom he had played in earlier years. One of them was the great Australian batsman, Don Bradman. "I remember shaking his hand and not washing mine for a week afterwards."

Home was young Katharine Worsley's great love. After leaving school she worked for a while in St Stephen's Orphanage in York, not wishing to move away from the county in which she had grown up. After that she taught in London – but enjoyed the long school holidays which would allow her to return to her "beloved Yorkshire". At that stage, she said, "I hoped music would be my life. I don't think I had any other real ambitions."

Then, when she was twenty-four, she met a certain young army officer stationed near the Worsleys' home in Catterick. I asked her how that had come about.

"We met at a private party, actually, not in Yorkshire. It was a strange meeting. I'd heard a lot about him. I'd read a lot about him in the papers. We became friends very quickly and, of course, with him being stationed near my home in Yorkshire, he was able to come over often. For the first time in his life he began to realise that there was such a thing called the country."

The Duke of Kent, who lost his own father when he was six, came to love Sir William Worsley very dearly. "He gained another father, I think," explained the Duchess. "My father played an enormous part in his life. I think he would say himself that it was my father who taught him what the countryside was all about." I had read that the Duke was attracted to his future wife because she wasn't excessively deferential. Had she, I asked, teased him a little? Her Royal Highness laughed. "I wouldn't be surprised."

The couple fell in love and wanted to marry. But they were considered too young and were asked to wait. The Duchess went abroad for a while. "I suppose to think it out, as I might have done on my desert island. And during that time I think it made us both quite certain that it was the right thing." The separation, however, was painful. "It was a long time," she remembered. "But I'm sure it was a wise thing to do." Romance survived the separation. The Duke went to Germany with his regiment, the woman he loved much further afield, to Canada. They were not great letter-writers, preferring to talk to each other on the phone. Four years later they were married in York Minster. It was 8 June 1961. And the Duchess would be quite happy to do it all over again.

"It was all a dream. I couldn't believe what was happening. The church that I knew so well, where I'd played the organ, suddenly was transformed with television lights and I just rather did what I was told that day. An extraordinary day. A very wonderful day, and the sun came out in the afternoon. It rained all morning, it rained all evening, but the sun came out in the afternoon. It was wonderful."

Her wedding dress had been specially commissioned from the London designer, John Cavanagh. He was the choice of her mother-in-law, Princess Marina. "She had extraordinary taste in dress and I was very happy to be dressed by her. I then had very little idea about what I liked in the way of clothes so I was lucky to have had her to train me."

Marriage transformed Katharine Worsley overnight from the private daughter of a distinguished Yorkshire family, into a royal duchess whose attention from the public was relentless. She was rarely out of the newspapers. Women copied the pageboy bob which she adopted as her hairstyle and followed her in wearing fashionable choker pearls. But, she says, she was unaware of this imitation. "I've always loved fashion and when we were first married I think the fashion I loved was very much for romantic, slightly old-fashioned clothes. I loved them – and I still do on certain occasions." But there was nothing particularly old-fashioned about the miniskirt which, I reminded her, she was the first member of the Royal Family to wear. "Funny you should know," she said, laughing. "I was seen in Oxford Street in a miniskirt. I remember it very, very well. It was not as 'mini' as they can be – but 'mini-er' than other members of my family had gone to at that stage." Had she been embarrassed by the incident, I asked. She said she hadn't – "but when I look back at the photographs of myself in those clothes now I can't believe I really did it". The young Duchess also wore long white Courrèges boots and became very much a trendsetter. She'd had no warning that her taste would attract so much publicity and it came as something of a shock. Once again, however, her mother-in-law was on hand to help. "Princess Marina was wonderful to me, and an enormous source of endless advice and encouragement."

On many occasions, the Duchess of Kent was voted one of the world's best-dressed women, rather as today the Princess of Wales has been. I asked her whether she thought the Princess's role had similarities to her own experience. She agreed it had. "We're all working for the same ideals," she explained.

It was the ideals of the Royal Family that we turned to next. The Duchess told me that when she becomes a patron of an organisation she tries very hard to work for it and not just be a symbolic member of it. Her work for the Samaritans is a good example of this. She did the course, trained properly and worked at St Stephen, Walbrook, for a short time.

"I enjoyed it enormously. And then the things I was being asked to do grew in number and I found that I couldn't simply go every Wednesday morning, as I was doing. And it was with a great sadness that I actually stopped doing it. But the course taught me an enormous amount about life. I mean, if you're going to spend quite a few months talking to people who may have suicidal tendencies, probably because they're lonely, you do begin to understand people and their problems and look at people in the street in a different way. You wonder what their problems are. You don't just take them all for granted."

The Duchess also works for Age Concern. "I love old people. I think that old age should be the happiest time in your life. And sadly, in reality, it very rarely is." She also visits hospices – perhaps the most difficult and demanding of all the work she does. She finds no problem, however, in meeting and talking to people who are dying. "The ones who are ill are the ones who give you confidence to talk to them. That is the most remarkable part of hospice work. They give to you so much more than you can ever give to them."

This concern for those who are ill was brought out very strongly in the next record Her Royal Highness chose. It was Jacqueline du Pré playing the Elgar Cello Concerto.

"I met Jacquie. Funnily enough we were never even introduced. It was at the Woman of the Year lunch, quite a long time ago. She was in her wheelchair already and she was wheeled past me and I just said 'Hello' and she said 'Hello' to me as if we'd known each other all our lives. And we formed a wonderful friendship. At the beginning she was either called Smiley or Jacquie because she was always laughing, always happy. She was a very, very lovely person and I visited her most weeks. She got weaker very quickly. I think I was very lucky to have been with her just a few hours before she died. I was able to share a few of those last moments with her."

Elgar's great Cello Concerto carried us naturally to the other aspect of the Duchess's life which gives her great joy – her work in music. She's a member of the Bach Choir, for which she has to re-audition every three years. "It's something none of us looks 'forward to'. It can be terrifying: I'd rather make a speech than audition." She's also patron of the BBC's Young Musician of the Year Competition and the Leeds Piano Competition, and President of the Royal Northern College of Music. It's work she loves – particularly going to Manchester to visit the Royal Northern College. "I'm just terribly proud of it. I love the feeling of belonging to it. I failed to qualify for a college of music myself and I've always longed to be part of something where everybody in the same building is there for one reason and one reason alone – they love music."

We had dwelled for quite a while on the careful, dutiful side of royalty. It was time, I thought, to ask some questions about the lighter side of life. How did she forget about her cares?

"I have a passion for the Greek Islands. I would walk and gradually learn more about Greece, its history and its people. If I could go there every year and swim, I'd be really happy. I love swimming in those waters – clear, lovely waters, rather cold." She also enjoys wind-surfing, although she doesn't think she's very good at it, and enjoys cycling a bit. She plays tennis once a week. The whole world, I reminded her, associates her with this game. After all, to most people she's the 'lady from Wimbledon'. This, she admitted, was quite a problem for her. American tourists surround her whenever she's in public immediately after the tournament has finished. "I think that many people imagine that I stand in the Centre Court throughout the year holding that plate and waiting for the new winner to come up and take it away from me."

Before I asked her to choose her final record, the Duchess told me about her book and her luxury. They were both distinctly practical. "I've decided to take the *Reader's Digest Do-It-Yourself Manual*. I'm going to build a raft and it would tell me how to do that. And I'm going to construct a fishing-net – and it would tell me how to do that too." And the luxury? Again, it was very useful. "I think I'd like a solar-powered lamp so that I can have light in the darkness and, of course, read through the long, dark nights."

With that and Mozart's 'Ave verum corpus', her favourite record which she had kept until the end, our programme together finished. Royalty has to protect itself. There are things which members of the Royal Family cannot, and probably should not, say. To that extent, the Duchess of Kent had not been as revealing about herself as some of my other castaways. But then no one expected that. Even so she had said enough, I thought, to tell us a lot about the young Yorkshire girl who became one of the most elegant women in the land. She had told us, too, that in being refined you do not have to be remote. Indeed, I thought I sensed that at times she found her royal position a little constricting. The picture of the Royal Highness happily fishing from the side of her home-made raft in the clear waters of an undiscovered island was one that came to mind too easily to be dismissed as altogether fantastic.

HRH The Duchess of Kent

Piano Sonata in D, K284 (Mozart)
Symphony No. 6, 'Pathétique' (Tchaikovsky)
Tuba Tune (Norman Cocker) – Francis Jackson (organ of York Minster)
Double Violin Concerto (Bach)
'Che gelida manina' from *La Bohème* (Puccini)
Cello Concerto (Elgar) – Jacqueline du Pré
Maxwell's Silver Hammer – The Beatles
Ave verum corpus (Mozart)

Book: *Reader's Digest New Do-It-Yourself Manual*

Luxury: *A solar-powered lamp*

GERALD SCARFE

I had interviewed Gerald Scarfe's wife before I recorded a programme with him. Jane Asher had been one of my first guests and so I had assumed that if I could get on with her, as I had done, then there was no reason why I couldn't get on with her husband. I was almost right. Gerald Scarfe and I did get on. But I'm not sure that he relished the experience all that much. He is one of those people who doesn't like being interviewed because he doesn't much enjoy talking about himself. It's the job of an interviewer to smooth away such misgivings – but I feel that in this case I failed. I don't think the programme was quite the special event I would have liked to have made it. I still don't know why: does he, I wonder?

That said, what he told me about his life and his work was wonderfully interesting. I think that explains something too. Good programmes are often enjoyable – for both the interviewer and the person being interviewed – but not always. Just as in writing, the best work can come slowly or painfully, so in radio, the things worth listening to sometimes have a difficult birth.

"I am sure I would try to escape from my island. I don't
like anywhere I am."

Gerald Scarfe is tall, dark and handsome to outward view. But what is he like on the inside? "I'm gnarled," he said. "I find things disturbing and my drawings depict that." The disturbance within does not manifest itself in any obvious way: Gerald Scarfe is not a man to carry on in an 'artistic' manner. "I don't rant and rave in restaurants as people expect artists to do," he said. "I think they're a bit disappointed that I don't stand on the table and shout at everybody." I can understand their surprise, if not their disappointment. Scarfe's drawings are monstrous caricatures, reflecting the world in a distorted, sometimes frightening, way. Yet Scarfe himself appears calm, balanced and well-behaved, enjoying a happy life with his wife, Jane Asher, and their children in a comfortable house by the River Thames in London. Inevitably I wanted to find the bridge that linked the man to his work.

Gerald Scarfe learned to draw as a solitary child bedridden with asthma. It was the one thing he could do apart from reading. He didn't have many friends – "children don't like to play with sick children, they want to be out and about kicking footballs around" – so drawing became his way of expressing himself. He remembers being asked by a teacher why he always drew disasters – and confesses that he was fond of apocalyptic pictures like mines collapsing, volcanoes erupting, natives uprising and ships sinking. "I think they were just things I was worried about." To understand Gerald Scarfe, you have to understand his worries. His twisted and fantastic pictures may be the product of a mind that's a little bit gnarled, but they don't belong to someone who is in favour of the sense of violence or unease he may portray. "I think people misunderstand when they see my drawings," he said. "They feel that I'm advocating violence and misery. I'm not. I'm crying out against it. I want it to stop. I've had enough of it. I'm frightened of it."

Gnarled, worried, frightened, disturbed – these seem to be recurring words in Gerald Scarfe's vocabulary, and yet I still could not detect such characteristics in the man himself. But those childhood drawings of disasters were obviously very good. He won a national art competition organised by a boys' comic. The runner-up was one David Hockney from Bradford!

We turned to an examination of his childhood: "I was a hunchback. I'd spend perhaps a week in bed and then I'd be up for a few days, then I'd collapse again with more asthma. There weren't the sophisticated drugs that there are now and so I was continually in bed, and I spent a lot of time in hospital as well. I remember being in lots of adult wards, and seeing some horrific things there. It was very frightening."

That word again. And with it the recognition that to be frightened, or to see frightening things, can become a natural part of life. "Children accept everything. To me, it was just my life. Only by comparison with other children could I see that I was different." He did no sport – his parents were frightened that it would aggravate his illness – and he was treated very much as an invalid. At the same time he was paraded in front of a succession of doctors, all of whom tried out their patent methods of recovery on the bewildered boy.

"I was rabbit-punched on the neck by some chap in South Kensington. I was douched in France with this arsenic water, bathed in it, drank it, did everything possible with it. And another man thought that I wasn't swallowing properly and gave me a plate to wear so I had to swallow properly. But none of it seemed to do any good."

One cure did work – even if it was rather brutal.

"There was a doctor in Harley Street who said to my father, 'When he has the next attack, bring him here.' My father duly rang, but to say I could hardly sit up in bed, let alone come there. The doctor said, 'Put him in a taxi and bring him here.' So my father did. He carried me to the taxi and took me to Harley Street, and when I arrived the doctor had moved his consulting room from the ground floor to the top floor on purpose. So I had to walk up all these stairs. When I got to the top I was absolutely at death's door. And the doctor said, 'Lie down on the couch and breathe carefully.' He just placed his fingers on my chest and within about three minutes I was perfectly normal. It was like magic. So it's also a very psychological disease. I don't know what that doctor did, I've never been able to work it out. But one moment I was at death's door and the next I was walking out of Harley Street with perfect good health."

Gerald Scarfe's asthma stopped when he began to get more independent. He left home at the age of nineteen and the necessity of having to look after himself seemed to fend off his illness. He still gets it, more mildly than he used to, and he's now protected by modern drugs, but it still occurs in a way that he cannot always predict and will probably never fully understand.

I found the story of Gerald Scarfe's childhood fascinating. It seemed to explain so much about him. I began to understand how childhood sickness can encourage external control while fuelling the imagination. The contrast between outward discipline and inner turmoil was already much easier to grasp.

His career as a cartoonist began with *Punch*, who paid him seven guineas a time for joky drawings about mothers-in-law lying in wait with rolling-pins and similar themes. But he soon tired of these and began to feel that he could make social comments through his drawings. The opportunity to do this regularly came through his association with *Private*

Eye. There he found the freedom to express himself as he wished, drawing what he liked and learning for the first time the art of political satire. But the magazine did not itself encourage him to be politically vicious. "I think that came out naturally. They just said, 'We want to have a drawing of Harold Wilson on the front cover looking at the Denning Report or something' – and then I would go on from there." For the first time, he says, he felt he had arrived somewhere he belonged. The people he worked with – Richard Ingrams, Auberon Waugh and Peter Cook – all came from a public school background very different from his own, but he still felt a kind of kinship with them. "We were all doing the same thing," he said.

It was through *Private Eye* that Gerald Scarfe met Jane Asher. As his wife, she is the person who is asked to react immediately to his work, to give as he calls it a "man in the street" opinion. She's never stopped him from drawing anything: indeed, she'd encouraged him to try and sell his originals, telling him that the idea of being an artist is that you paint paintings and then sell them – you don't put them in a drawer. But for a long time Scarfe was reluctant to do this. He'd been told while working for the *Daily Mail* that he had to have a policy of selling all his original work or none of it and had decided against allowing any of it to reach the market. Now, however, you can buy original Scarfes at auction. His picture of 'Nanny Thatcher' – Mrs Thatcher spooning out bad medicine – went for £4,000 and one of 'Inflation' – Nigel Lawson inflating – reached a similar price. He himself has no favourites. "Once I've done them, I don't want to see them again. I don't usually have them hanging in the home because it reminds me of what I've just done. I've always felt that time is short, partly because of my childhood, I'm sure. I feel as though I'm behind in everything and I must get on. Anything that impedes my eye, like a drawing hanging on the wall, would make me think in the wrong direction."

Here was another clue to Scarfe's character and one that again stemmed from his childhood. He may be used to solitude but that has not prevented him from being ruthless. He is capable of viewing what he has done as a barrier to what he might do next and this impatience would accompany him to the desert island. "I'm not very good at sitting still. I'm a continual traveller. I don't really like going on holiday very much because I've got no patience when I'm there. I'm sure I would try and escape from the island. I don't like anywhere I am."

Gerald Scarfe's cartoon technique has a name. It's called transmogrification – the art of turning people into things. I asked him how he got his ideas for this. Was it something that struck him immediately – or did he take time to develop an idea?

"It's something that sometimes strikes me immediately. I generally draw Mrs Thatcher as a rather sharp implement, perhaps an axe or a sword.

I might see Nigel Lawson as a spongy doughnut – they automatically suggest themselves as that. But I think transmogrification for me is a way of avoiding the boredom of the job because if you can imagine drawing Mrs Thatcher over and over and over again, which I have done, it is incredibly boring. So, I think, just to please myself I try and turn her into a tank or an old boot."

So it's boredom that has turned Enoch Powell into a terrible Union Jack and transformed Harold Macmillan into Christine Keeler. The Macmillan picture was actually the one which set Gerald Scarfe on the path he has taken since. It made him realise what he could do with his drawings because it created such tremendous interest at the time.

Scarfe feels no personal animosity towards those whom he depicts, nor does he always assume the editorial policy of the newspaper for which he is working. He creates his own. He's not the least bit pompous about this attitude and brushed aside any notion of mine that it reflected his journalistic integrity. It's a human, artistic position. "I wouldn't want a drawing that I didn't believe in to be printed."

This highly personal approach to his work affected him deeply when, while working for the *Daily Mail*, he was sent to Vietnam. He found it a very difficult experience.

"I think they probably thought 'a grotesque artist for a grotesque situation'. But I found there, for the first time, that I was unable to draw what I found because up until then I'd been drawing abstract ideas, ideas from my own imagination. When I got there I found out that it really meant women and children caught up in a war that they didn't understand."

While in Vietnam he felt obliged to draw everything and even went to try and work in the morgue at the airport in Saigon. "I just couldn't cope with it," he said. "It had never struck me before that when men are shot in battle they're blown into bits. The morgue was full of bits and pieces, torsos without heads, legs – just bits of people. I remember gripping my armpits and sweating like mad. I couldn't draw in there at all." Up until that moment, reality had not intruded upon the artist's mental picture. For him the war had been – as it had for millions of others – a television event and he had reacted to it as such. The human agony which he found left him stranded: there is no technique for overcoming despair. By the time the *Sunday Times* sent him to draw the cholera epidemic in Calcutta he'd managed to come to terms with the artist as reporter, even though here, too, he found the situation difficult.

"I was amongst all these people dying in a hospital and I thought, This is a terrible invasion of privacy. Yet the photographer that I'd gone with was clicking away merrily with his Nikon and I thought, Of course, that's what I'm here to do really. *I'm* to report the situation, so that either we can put a stop to it or they can send some money or whatever and help the situation. And I then began to draw, and of course, once I begin to draw, it takes over and I'm concerned with how to get it right. To a certain extent the humanity leaves me.''

These days Scarfe is not only an artist and cartoonist, but a designer as well. He's had great success, particularly with the English National Opera's production of Offenbach's *Orpheus in the Underworld*. One review, he reminded me, said, 'Never work with children, animals and Gerald Scarfe'. He's enjoyed his success in this field very much and finds it a great antidote to the loneliness of his studio. He finds it exhilarating to watch people react to his paintings with laughter. ''Jane always says I'm very much a showbiz artist. I want reaction. I want applause.''

When Gerald Scarfe draws himself, he looks ''haggard, gaunt, very dark'' and has ''worried whirling eyes with deep, bushy eyebrows and a long pendulous jowl and down-turned mouth''. If *Desert Island Discs* were a television programme I cannot imagine that he would get away with such a description. But radio kept the secret of how he really looks and gave him a book by Capability Brown to help him redesign the island's layout and a picture by Turner to remind him of the Thames that flows past his home.

I'm not sure that I ever put a foot on the bridge between Scarfe the artist and Gerald Scarfe the man. But then, perhaps, it's not a journey I should have been allowed to make.

Gerald Scarfe

Bless You for Being an Angel – The Ink Spots
La mer – Charles Trenet
Art Gallery (sketch) – Peter Cook and Dudley Moore
Nocturne in E flat Op. 9 No. 2 (Chopin)
Cello Suite No. 1 in G (Bach)
Prologue to *Under Milk Wood* (Dylan Thomas) – Richard Burton
The penultimate scene of *Don Giovanni* (Mozart)
Prelude to Act 1 of *Die Walküre* (Wagner)

Book: *A Book by Capability Brown*

Luxury: *A river painting by Turner*

JOAN ARMATRADING

Joan Armatrading's ambition is to write a song that will live for ever. Some would say that she has done that already with 'Love and Affection'. The singer herself seems less certain. Posterity, she feels, should be given a wider choice and she keeps working to ensure its availability. For this reason, work is very important to her, and fills her life to the exclusion of many other things.

I thought we were very lucky when I heard that she had agreed to appear on *Desert Island Discs*. Joan Armatrading is someone who protects her privacy passionately and I fully expected her to refuse our invitation. But the lure of the radio island worked its magic once again, and she came to the studio to talk about her life and share her musical tastes with me. Of the eight records, four were classical: Mendelssohn, Mahler, Dvořák and Verdi all found a place in her selection. They did so quite naturally. There is no pretension in Joan Armatrading and she is an unassuming, simple and sincere person. She displays none of the arrogance of the pop star and dislikes fame for its own sake. She exudes a tremendous belief in herself and in her talent. While she enjoys applause, she prefers appreciation. While she acknowledges the clamour of the crowd, she knows that her work will only survive if its quality is good enough. It is these things which make her an artist rather than a star.

"I think a desert island would actually suit me."

Joan Armatrading likes nothing better than being alone. "I think a desert island would actually suit me. It took me quite a while to get used to people. When I was younger, growing up, I did lots of things on my own. I didn't have a bunch of friends. I was an observer. I'd always be the one standing in the playground looking at everyone else. It didn't bother me. I was very happy." She spoke in the past tense – but wasn't it true that she was still like that? "Not as bad." She laughed. "I try and mix a little bit more but I'm still told that I don't mix as much as I ought to. But sometimes it's very difficult not to be disappointed with people."

Isolation, she explained, provides her with the antidote to popular success. "When I go on tour my favourite time is after the show when I've played in front of thousands of people – which is brilliant, I love that – but when I go to my room it's just me on my own." She wouldn't miss people. She wouldn't miss television. She wouldn't miss the radio. She wouldn't miss her car. There's no doubt about it. Our desert island was made for Joan Armatrading.

She came to Britain at the age of seven, travelling by herself from Antigua, with a sign round her neck saying who she was and where she was bound. She was coming to Birmingham to join her mother and father who had left the Caribbean one by one to start a new life in the industrial Midlands. She had four brothers and one sister. She can still remember getting off the bus at New Street in Birmingham and the pleasure of seeing her mother again. Not long after that she saw snow for the first time. It was "brilliant – I was just in it, I loved it". Apart from that, however, she remembers life as being quite normal. "My parents didn't say: 'Well, Joan, you're black and those guys are white – have you noticed?'" Race was not a big issue for her – and that's how it has remained.

"I tend to look at people as people. I am aware of the colour of my skin and I like it. I think it's great. A lot of colours suit it. You can wear black and that looks great and red really shines. But apart from that I don't see it as an issue for myself. I'm not saying that it's not a problem for some people and it's not something to tackle but sometimes I do feel people carry a chip and say, 'It's because I'm black'. And it's not. It's probably because somebody just doesn't like you."

Music entered Joan Armatrading's life when her mum bought a piano. To begin with the whole family – mother, father and six children – had lived in one room. But then two families left the house and suddenly there was new-found space which needed filling up. The answer was a piano "to put in the posh front room". Mother thought it would look nice, which it did. It was just a piece of furniture. Then Joan started to play it.

"I just started out playing my own stuff. My dad used to have a guitar – he used to sit on the step and play 'Blue Moon', sort of a jazz style, which sounded great. But that was the only thing he could play that I remember, and I think maybe hearing him play made me want to play the guitar. But he didn't want me to play his guitar, so he used to hide it."

Undaunted, Joan spotted a guitar in a local pawnshop. It cost three pounds but her mother, whom she badgered to let her have it, could not afford so much. However, she did have two old prams. If the woman in the pawnshop would swap two old prams for a guitar, Joan could have what she wanted. The deal was done – and Joan Armatrading got her first guitar.

From then on, she became her own songwriter. While other kids became fans of the Beatles or Gerry and the Pacemakers, Joan Armatrading preferred her own material. When her chance came to perform in public, however, it was a well-known song that she chose. Her brother was helping to organise a concert at Birmingham University and invited her to sing. All she knew were the numbers she had written herself – but her brother didn't feel that would go down well. Instead, she gave her audience Simon and Garfunkel's 'The Sound of Silence'. "I was aware," she told me drily, "that it wasn't my favourite moment in history. But I did it."

Her first professional break came when she was nineteen. Pam Nestor, a friend, asked her to set one of her poems to music. Together they wrote a couple of other songs and with these, and the ones which Joan had written on her own, they were given a recording contract. After that came Joan's first album and things grew from there. In all of this, she never intended to become a performer: all she wanted was to be famous for writing songs.

"That would have been brilliant. I'd have loved it if I could have written songs and just have people record them and say 'That's a brilliant song, who wrote that?' I'm not an exhibitionist. But over the years I've started to dance about and really enjoy myself on-stage, and I look at my being on-stage as my night out. That's my club . . . That's my way of having, you know, a bit of fun."

Joan Armatrading's independence, and her refusal to make many concessions to glamour, have encouraged some people to try and brand her as a feminist symbol. It's not a position she particularly enjoys.

"Feminism is such a strange thing. I'm very much for equal opportunity, and I believe that if a woman is capable of doing the same job as a man she should have the right or the opportunity to prove that she can do it. But I'm not for bully tactics, and sometimes feminists come across as bullies to me. That's the part I don't like."

Just as she avoids the issue of feminism, so she doesn't like being drawn into general politics. Her world is one of emotion – "looking at people and seeing the different emotions and traumas they're going through. I notice when people are very happy in love – the way they look. And when they're miserable, the way they look. It's generally to do with love of something – love of work, love of money, love for another person. It's quite a strong emotion." How much of her work, I asked, was born of herself? Her answer was two-pronged: "I do write songs about myself", but then she reminded me she'd written thirteen albums, each with ten songs on it. "If you imagine that every single year I'm sitting there writing about Joan Armatrading – could that be more boring, or what?" Nevertheless, her songs do seem to contain a recurrent theme – a certain vulnerability and loneliness. Was that, I wondered, part of her? She told me no. "I'm not really a lonely sort of person." She could recall a time in her life when she was, but that had now passed. She hasn't got lots of friends because, as her classic song, 'Love and Affection', says: "I've got all the friends I want. I may need more but I'll stick to those I've got." She prefers a few friends she can trust. For the rest, her music keeps her company.

Her love of her work and her music has driven her hard. So much so that a couple of years ago it began to take a toll on her health. She decided she needed a break. "I didn't do anything. I just slept, drove around a bit, sat in the garden, watched a bit of television – but didn't play my guitar, didn't write and didn't listen to much music." Altogether she took a year off and for most of that time had nothing to do with music. After that she set about reorganising her life. She now tours for shorter periods – although she still travels for two months at a time – and plans to make fewer albums if she can. She's also bought a stud farm.

"I don't know anything about horses – four legs and a tail and a head, that's it. But I started to set up the stud farm hopefully to be a proper sort of business and not just a game. For some reason I sort of got into it, and then once you're in it, there's no stopping because you start to look at the animals as if they're people. And they're always sick. That's the one thing you learn about horses very quickly. They're always sick."

Alone with her sick horses and rarely seen in the social whirl, Joan Armatrading is far from being a typical rock star. One of her great passions, a hangover from that house in Birmingham, when she was kept busy with the cleaning a lot of the time, is housework. She loves hoovering. Two of her records, Mahler's fourth symphony and the Verdi *Requiem*, were both employed as "music to hoover by". She's also a very disciplined person – she doesn't smoke or drink – and she's a vegetarian as well. When she needs a pleasant interlude she turns to her comics. Every week she gets a large selection. "I read *Dandy, Beano, Mandy, Bunty, Judy, The Wizard, Sparky* (when that used to come out), *Topper, Beezer* – you name it, I'll read it. There's a black Superman in the African comics – so I try and get different things." And then, with a laugh, she added: "That's pretty exciting, don't you think?"

"How long does that take?" I asked, surprised that such a busy musician could find the time to wade through so many publications each week. "It depends," she replied. "Sometimes I read them really quickly – and sometimes I try and save them up. But I'm not always very good at doing that because I get excited and just have to get through them."

Her happiness to talk about such simple pleasures and her enjoyment of her own carefully structured world seemed to me to describe someone who felt herself being carried along by events. Was she, I asked, a fatalist?

"I think things seem to happen that you have absolutely no control over. There are certain things you can't plan. I didn't plan to get into the music business. Even when I did that first thing for my brother, I didn't do it and then think: 'Right: this is it. I'm off.' Even when I made my first record I still wasn't planning on doing what I've ended up doing. But once I was in it – then I was very happy and I made up my mind. Just get on with it, and enjoy it. And I do – very much."

For her book she chose Agatha Christie's *Why Didn't They Ask Evans?* Britain's most popular novelist had won by a short head, she admitted, over a large selection of comics. Her luxury, of course, was her guitar. As she told me her choices, she became enamoured of the whole idea. "I'm actually quite looking forward to this," she said. "When can I go?"

I'm not sure that she really would enjoy life on a desert island, but I know what she meant. For a little girl who travelled alone from the West Indies to Britain in the mid-fifties, the world in which Joan Armatrading found herself must have been startling and mystifying. However secure her family, she must have felt like an outsider looking in. Perhaps the discovery of a rich and deep musical talent within her only served to increase that sense of isolation. That's why her lovely songs come from a woman who stands apart, alone without being lonely, the contented observer who prefers to look rather than to join in. She doesn't need radio's desert island. She has her own territory here among her admirers at home.

Joan Armatrading

Violin Concerto in E minor (Mendelssohn)
That Old Black Magic – Ella Fitzgerald
Madame George – Van Morrison
Symphony No. 4 (Mahler)
The Magnificent Seven (theme music from the film)
'Dies irae' from *Requiem* (Verdi)
I'm a Man – Muddy Waters
Symphony No. 9, 'New World' (Dvořák)

Book: *Why Didn't They Ask Evans?*
(Agatha Christie)

Luxury: *A guitar*

A. WAINWRIGHT

Few castaways have proved as elusive as A. Wainwright. Like a walker disappearing into a Cumbrian mist, he was a difficult man to track down. Our negotiations with him were more complicated and protracted than those with Joan Collins or the Archbishop of Canterbury. For Wainwright is his own man, and life in the company of rugged countryside has made him sure-footed in his tastes.

We eventually caught up with him through a contact in the Lake District. After much deliberation the answer came back that he *would* consent to appear on *Desert Island Discs*, but only on certain conditions. To begin with, he wasn't coming to London. He'd been there once since the war, hadn't liked it and didn't intend to return. So we agreed to record the programme in the BBC's Manchester studios – but here, too, there was a condition. If Wainwright were to travel that far south (remember that if you live in the Lake District, Manchester is in the Midlands) his journey would have to include a detour to Harry Ramsden's famous fish-and-chip restaurant near Leeds. So the deal was done – and Wainwright consented to forsake the isolation of his beloved hills for the imagined loneliness of radio's desert island.

Wainwright's love for the Lake District and his knowledge of the dales and fells of northern England is now familiar to millions of readers. He is the constant companion of any serious walker in those parts. His books, written in his own hand and accompanied by careful pen-and-ink drawings and detailed maps, are not only attractive in their charm, but indispensable in their wisdom. There are many who don't feel properly equipped unless they've got a 'Wainwright' with them.

". . . the last time I did a fell walk the mountains wept
tears for me. It never stopped raining."

Wainwright is a mirror of the land he has made famous. He likes anonymity, enjoys being alone. He is a strong, solitary character, preferring silence to music, and his own thoughts to those of other people. "I am antisocial," he confessed. "I'm getting worse as I get older. It started as shyness, it isn't shyness now. I can face anybody now and not feel inferior to them, but I'd much rather be alone."

Now, however, there's an obvious problem. Wainwright's books are best-sellers, and have attracted people to the landscape he loves. Doesn't it worry him that he might have destroyed some of its peace?

"I've often been charged with that, but I don't think so – I certainly don't reproach myself about it. There's been such a change in leisure habits. When I started on the fells there were very few walkers there. Nowadays they walk in procession. But they would have come anyway because they've more money to spend, they've more leisure-time."

"But when you've ever met them, you've walked straight on?"

"I've tried to avoid them, yes."

This struck me as unusual. If two people meet in the middle of nowhere – or as near to nowhere as our small island allows – surely they have to greet each other. You couldn't just walk past each other in silence. Surely you've got to say *something*?

"No, you haven't really – you can strike off in another direction, there are boulders you can get behind. My pet hate, of course, is school parties, where you get a caterpillar of about forty kids coming along. You say 'Good morning' to the first one – but the rest of them have to share it. I'm not going to say it forty times."

Now there I have some sympathy. After all, toiling up hillsides is a breathless business at the best of times. I think a school party should be satisfied with one 'Good morning' between them.

Wainwright – he doesn't like to use his first name, Alfred, which, he says, is nice for a little boy "but doesn't suit a man" – caught the walking bug as a child growing up in Lancashire. He was born in Blackburn. His father was a travelling stonemason and the family was poor. Walking, he says, "was the only pastime we had when we were children".

"Nobody ever had a penny to spend, so we amused ourselves in ways that don't seem to appeal to children at all these days – we'd play hide-and-seek, we'd play marbles along the gutter, kick a rag ball about, collect cigarette cards – it was a wonderful life, really."

The poverty didn't matter because it was shared by so many others. "You never felt that you were poor because everybody else was in the same boat. People accepted the position. That's the way they were born."

But as things turned out, the young Alfred Wainwright was destined for a path rather different from his friends and neighbours. While the children with whom he played in the street ended up working in the local cotton mill, Wainwright was clever enough to take a different path.

"I did very well at the board school and the teachers all said you ought to go to the central school in the middle of the town, which I did with considerable apprehension, because I had no decent clothes to wear – no shoes. But there I did extremely well and came first in every subject in the first year."

But this early academic success did not prevent him from having to earn a living. "There wasn't much money coming in at home and I wanted to help out." So, at the age of thirteen, he applied for a job as an office boy in the town hall. He got it. Everybody else he knew was going into the cotton mill.

"I started at fifteen shillings a week and I remember running all the way home to tell my mother, who had a hard time – I used to wake up in the middle of the night and I could hear the mangle going in the kitchen downstairs because, to make ends meet, she had to take in washing from rather more affluent neighbours."

Wainwright continued to work in Blackburn for the next ten years. It wasn't until 1930, when he was twenty-three, that he took his first holiday away from home.

"I'd saved up five pounds, I'd heard a lot about the Lake District, which until then had been a world away although there were only sixty miles between us. So I did as everybody told me, went up to Orrest Head which overlooks Windermere. I just couldn't believe that such beauty could exist – it made the whole world of difference to me. That did change my life – I decided then that this was a place where I wanted to live. In 1941, I applied for a job in the town hall in Kendal, and got it."

And that was the beginning of the next part of his life. Once again, I was struck by the comparison between Wainwright's character and that of the natural world which he has inhabited. Born in a Lancashire cotton town in very poor circumstances, clever enough to improve his position just a little and then, having had a glimpse of where he'd like to be, slowly, inexorably heading here. It was like a patient walk up a mountain-side, rising slowly from undistinguished beginnings to a vantage point from which not only the summit, but the path towards it, is visible.

My next question was obvious. When had he decided on the project to write about the Lake District in such detail? He began, he said, more for his own amusement than anything else. Once installed in Kendal, he had a golden opportunity to get on to the fells. There weren't many people with the same idea in those days – but even so he was always coming across

123

people who were lost. A guidebook was needed, so he began to write one. "I thought, when I'm an old man and I can't walk the hills, these will be memories for me." He finished the first volume after two years of working on it every night.

"I really got obsessed by what I was doing. I was able to illustrate the fells with drawings, I was able to give features – the natural features of the mountains and the routes of ascent. Then I put in the ridge routes to the next one, the view from the summit. I've dealt with them all like that, one after another." When he'd finished he showed his work to a few people, all of whom told him he ought to get it published. That proved no easy task.

"Although I'd only £35 saved up, I went to a local printer and asked what it would cost to have 2,000 copies made, and he worked it out, and said £900. I said I'd only got £35. 'Well,' he said, 'never mind, this book will sell – pay me off as you sell them.' And he went ahead and printed them. Now that was a wonderful thing. That firm continued to publish me but were eventually taken over by the *Westmorland Gazette* who have published most of my books ever since. They've been a great friend to me. I wanted every page to be *exactly* as I had written it by hand so they were all photographed and that's how the first book came into being."

He had used the word 'obsessed' earlier. Had the books dominated his life completely?

"They did. Nothing mattered to me except getting these books done. I had a single-track mind. It ended finally with my wife walking out and taking the dog and I never saw her again."

"Did you blame her?"

"Not at all – I don't know how she stuck it for thirty-odd years. Right, what's your next question?"

I have to confess that my mind had gone rather blank. It's difficult to think of anything to say to a man who has told you so bluntly and unexpectedly about the collapse of his marriage. I am not ashamed to admit that I took refuge in the programme's format – "Let's have your next record". It turned out to be Pavarotti singing 'Come Back to Sorrento'. Hardly the most reflective melody with which to digest Wainwright's marital predicament. Perhaps that's why I forgot to ask him why his wife had taken the dog. Instead, I went back to walking and asked him what makes a good walker.

"I don't think there's any art about walking and I can't understand why you get tremendous volumes of books about 'how to walk'. It's a natural thing, but on the fells, which are quite rough, you must take care to watch where you're putting your feet. There's always a temptation to look at the view as you're walking along. You mustn't do that. That's the way accidents happen."

It all sounded very methodical – head down, plodding along, not daring to look at the view lest you fall over the edge. But that's Wainwright – one minute matter-of-fact and rather down, the next surprising, even poetic, as he described what it was like to sleep out alone on the fells.

"It's eerie. There's absolute silence and all around the mountains are just black silhouettes. Then, gradually, you get the grey dawn. The valleys are filled with a white vapour and you watch it gradually dissolve and reveal the fields and pastures below. It's a wonderful experience. Always alone, you know that you're the only person on the fells that morning – like a king, wandering where you like, this is my throne, and knowing that for four or five hours you've got the fells to yourself to wander just where you like and nobody else will appear on the scene."

Wainwright the king, alone on the hills – it made a curious but nonetheless appealing picture. He struck me in that moment as a mixture of crusty clichés and true romanticism and this was reinforced by the remarks he made after he'd chosen his next record, 'Oh What a Beautiful Mornin'' from *Oklahoma!* "What a wonderfully inspiring song! And you notice, he sings about the sounds of the earth being like music. Now that's the sort of music that I *really* prefer – the tinkle of a mountain stream, the twittering of birds, the rustle of leaves in a forest in autumn, the sound of the wind sighing across the mountaintops – that's music to me. And there's never any discord, it's harmony."

Alfred Wainwright doesn't walk any more. He's over eighty now and his eyes are going. He lives with his second wife, Betty, writing and looking after animals rescued through the good offices of a charity called the Wainwright Animal Trust which he established with the money he had earned from his books. He doesn't take any royalties for his work – but leaves his publishers to distribute them at their discretion to animal charities which he supports. All this keeps him busy – but it's a far cry from tramping through those precious, life-giving fells. He told me about his last walk.

"It was a pouring wet day, terrible wet day, and I was stumbling and slipping all over the place, and it wasn't because my glasses were misted, it was because I couldn't see where I was putting my feet. That's the last time I did a fell walk – and the mountains wept tears for me that day. It never stopped raining."

For all that he's a man with a deep and forceful love of nature, Wainwright remains unmoved by thoughts of God. "I've no time at all for organised religion. I can't believe that we go to heaven or hell." He cannot concede that the splendid scenery which he has made the backdrop to his life is anyway God-given. "It's a mystery that nobody's ever solved. It really is a wonderful world, a beautiful world. I'm sure that somebody's created it, but I don't know who." That, I thought, is typical Wainwright.

A life in close proximity to impressive things had made him a man very difficult to impress.

He'd asked me at the start of the programme whether there was a chip shop on the island and I'd had to disappoint him. "In that case," he now told me, "I haven't a great deal of time to spend before I fade away." There seemed little prospect of cheering him up. He didn't even want the normal ration of Shakespeare and the Bible, let alone anything else. "I wouldn't want either of those because I couldn't read them," he said (referring to his failing eyesight). "I wouldn't want a book at all." But, he said, "I've always had an ambition to grow a beard and I'd never be able to face people and their comments if I tried to do it now – but on a desert island it would be ideal. So I'd like a small mirror, just to see how it was getting on." It seemed a very small luxury. Was there anything else? Yes, indeed, there was : "The other things I would take would be two photographs – one of the Blackburn Rovers football team that won the FA Cup in 1928 – that was really a highlight of my life – and the second would be of my wife, Betty, who's been a treasure to me, and continues to be."

It was a difficult request to refuse. Wainwright was obviously not looking forward to his bookless, chipless existence on the desert island. If a small mirror and a couple of photographs would make it more bearable, he should have them.

We had finished as idiosyncratically as we had begun. As we parted, he back to Kendal and me to London, I had a picture of this remarkable, enduring old man sitting alone on an island with only two pictures and an advancing beard for company. And then I thought of the visions that would fill his head: of sunny valleys and rolling mists, of happy bubbling streams and grim grey slabs of rock. All these and more would always be Alfred Wainwright's companions – wherever he happened to be.

A. Wainwright

Tales from the Vienna Woods (J. Strauss II) – Richard Tauber

Smoke Gets in Your Eyes – Tommy Dorsey and His Orchestra

There's an Empty Cot in the Bunkhouse Tonight – Rex Allen

Come Back to Sorrento – Luciano Pavarotti

Oh, What a Beautiful Mornin' (*Oklahoma!*) – Gordon MacRae

The Happy Wanderer – Berkshire Boys Choir

Skye Boat Song – Kenneth McKellar

Somewhere My Love ('Lara's Theme' from
Dr Zhivago) – Johnny Mathis

Book: *No book, but two photographs – one of the 1928 Blackburn Rovers football team, the other of his wife, Betty*

Luxury: *A mirror (to watch his beard growing)*

LUCINDA LAMBTON

I felt as if we had already made a programme with Lucinda Lambton by the time we sat down to record it. She arrived late and in a state of some disarray. She'd had great difficulty in reducing the list of records from her original selection of eighteen down to eight. On the appointed day she had managed, through a Herculean effort of self-censorship, to whittle it down to thirteen. But beyond that it would not go. So we spent an hour helping her to make a final selection. Should we include the Finkenberger Trio singing a yodelling song – or did we prefer a very old recording of 'La Marseillaise'? Which appealed more – 'A Four-legged Friend' or 'The Runaway Train'? Lucy Lambton encouraged us to make these agonising decisions with her by marching round the studio humming, singing – and even yodelling – to each of the records. Brahms, Bellini and Monteverdi were among those reluctantly cast aside when we at last found ourselves ready to begin the programme.

Lucinda Lambton's inability to complete her choice stemmed from an anxiety to do the interview well. She regarded it as very important: she considered it an honour to be asked. At the same time, modesty had convinced her that nobody would find her interesting – a view reinforced by her determination not to talk about her personal life and background at all.

She could not have been more wrong. This edition of *Desert Island Discs* enjoyed a marvellous popular reaction. The audience, like the interviewer, were charmed by her enthusiasm and impressed by her energy. They also knew her to be serious and honest, as valuable to our history as the forgotten ancestors she disentombs.

"There are thousands more secrets in the English countryside
– thousands upon thousands, billions and trillions
more . . ."

Lucinda Lambton is the epitome of that great English characteristic – love of the unusual. She has converted the country in which she lives into a world of exploration. Its mysteries are her delight and, as a result, her catalogue of discoveries is long – ranging from the smug self-importance of Victorian lavatories at one end to the zany inconsequentialities of eighteenth-century follies at the other. None of this makes her eccentric. In fact, it's a word she hates – "a stupid, idiotic word" – and she takes her work seriously. But "serious things with a laugh are twice the value" and that's how she approaches everything she does. She does many things and has many passions.

She's most passionate about her children – and then dogs, buildings and people. Showing off buildings and showing off excitements all over the country – "that thrills me to absolute fever-pitch day in and day out, year in and year out". Strange things catch her eye. She is irresistibly drawn to such curiosities as a monument to commemorate a pig in Cornwall or a memorial to a balloon in Bedford. "They make me roar with laughter," she explained, "and give me the thrill of excitement at discovering them. What could be more delightful than chancing upon the information that Lady Mount Edgcumbe kept a pet pig called Cupid which, tethered to a gold chain, she took down to breakfast, lunch, tea and dinner – and also on outings to London? And when it died, she had it buried in a golden casket and put a huge soaring stone obelisk over its head. What could be more delightful than that?" Delightful, certainly, but to spend your life exploring such things seemed quite a large decision, I thought. "It wasn't really a decision," replied Lucy Lambton. "I was just swept along at an uncontrollable, thundering pace."

The desert island would offer respite from all that. "It's welcome to be able to gather everything together and rest for a moment or two. It would be lovely. An enforced rest would be a delight." In the meantime, however, there is work to be done, work to which she is utterly dedicated. She once swam across to an island with a saw between her teeth so that she could cut away undergrowth that was spoiling her photograph. "I also disrobed because I didn't want to get my clothes wet," she added. "Embarrassing – because the world and his wife were picnicking. But there was this lovely Gothic duck-house on the island. It was the only way, because you couldn't see it. I knew it was there."

Such dedication is by no means always pleasurable – "Setting up a picture is hours of pain." The pleasure comes in the act of exploration itself – "thundering around England and meeting people – that's pleasure. Pure, pure pleasure."

Lucy Lambton uses the word 'thunder' a lot. Her exhilaration for what she does is a great wave sweeping her across Britain in her search for its curious mementos. Occasionally the waters recede to leave her beached in some most unpleasant places. Like Britain's lavatories, whose historical development she had bravely decided to photograph. "It was foul – sodden with Gumption and sodden cloths and lavatory brushes. It was horrible, really horrible. The car became as aromatic as the lavatories themselves. And being underground in those lavatories with the lights on bringing out the aroma to an absolute pitch seven hours, twelve hours. Once I was fourteen hours underground in the public lavatories in Hull." Greater love hath no photographer. There can only be one question: Why? "Because I realised, having seen the gents' urinals in the Philharmonic at Liverpool, which were pink marble, pretending marble, it was put on with sponges – how many lavatories were repellent all over the country. I saw that they should go, and they therefore should be recorded before they went. And then, of course, I found out they'd been invented in England, sort of within living memory – the first proper working lavatory was little more than a hundred years ago."

I wasn't quite sure that the question had been answered completely. And anyway, wasn't it the Ancient Greeks who invented lavatories? "Yes, yes, yes," replied Lucy, irritated by my pedestrian approach to the history of these things. "I'm talking about the ballcocks and valves and all the flushing business." That explained it. We could drop the subject – particularly since lavatories no longer interest their heroic photographer. "I hate them," she said. "I don't know why I'm getting up such a fever of excitement talking to you about them. I loathe them."

Lucy Lambton is not only a collector of things. She collects people too. She once collected Bing Crosby. It happened when she was seventeen. "That was exciting. Very, very exciting. Going out into the street in London and seeing him walking along and stopping him and saying, 'I live in that house, can you come to lunch?' And he came. And my mother was up a ladder pruning roses. She was the greatest, I suppose, fan that Bing Crosby had. She was standing on the top of the ladder and I said, 'Oh, do you know Bing Crosby?' and she turned, and there was the Old Groaner himself with a straw hat on and smoking a pipe. It was a terrifying shock for her. Anyway, there he was, and he stayed for lunch and he was absolutely delightful."

Later in life she collected Yuri Gagarin, the Russian astronaut who became the first man in space. This, she admitted, wasn't "really exciting" – but it's a lovely story all the same. One of her first jobs had been to follow him round the country taking photographs of his visit to Britain. "There was one moment of crowning glory when he was leaving Heathrow. He walked up this great, long, red carpet and came off the carpet and walked over and gave me a deep bow. And then he walked back on the carpet and on to the aeroplane. It was a moment of glorious triumph. It was simply that he had seen my face about the places he'd toured in England. I suppose he thought I was a person of consequence, because I'd always been there." After Bing Crosby and Yuri Gagarin came the Everly Brothers – proving that Lucy Lambton's taste in people is as eclectic as her taste in things. She found herself sharing an overnight railway journey from King's Cross to Edinburgh with the Everlys and Buddy Holly's backing group, the Crickets. "We sat in those small sleeper compartments all night, playing guitars and singing away until four or five in the morning. All scrunched into a tiny sleeper, all the way to Edinburgh." She has stayed friends with them ever since. "It has strange consequences now," she said. She can be going along with her ordinary life and then, when they come to England, she's suddenly "plunged into a life of sailing around London in black stretch-limos waving at fans".

To a certain extent it's lack of formal education which has made Lucy Lambton tireless in her pursuit of information. She left school very young – at about thirteen. "I can't remember exactly what date, but certainly too early for comfort. I've ground my teeth in rage that I wasn't properly educated. I'd like to have been. It would have been a joy." It worries her – "constantly, daily, hourly. I feel as if I'm always dealing with picked flowers rather than flowers that are actually planted – any new information hasn't got the right foundation because it's gathered anew on the surface. Another thing about not having been thoroughly educated is that when you read or hear of something you're not always able to connect it to something else. You get things in isolation all the time. I find that agony."

She was born in Durham – and the North-East of England remains very important to her. Rather than choose a Geordie song to take to her desert island she decided that she could always sing one instead – and gave me a rendering of 'The Bladon Races' just to prove it. She had four sisters and a brother – all much younger than she was. She worshipped dogs and, from the age of eleven, horses. "I loved the competition of potato races, obstacle races and musical chairs. Oh, I loved them so much."

Today, however, Lucy Lambton is the nation's snapper-up of unconsidered Victoriana. She's helped to save a beautiful swimming bath – "built as the town hall in Siena" – and campaigned against such things as the pulling down of old buildings on the east side of Trafalgar Square. "I don't play a major part," she said. "I simply provide the photographs." But that, I suspect, is a rather deprecating description of her rôle. Her pictures are undeniably valuable: her enormous enthusiasm and commitment must be priceless. It takes her to some odd places. "It's so delightful ferreting things out and knowing, as you drive along, what's behind a wall and what's over a field. I drove up the M5 yesterday and knew that a lady was lying in the churchyard who died in 1840, having had thirty children, all of whom had died in infancy except for one who died when he was two. And knowing she was there as the rain fell was so magical. I love that – knowing the ins and outs all over England."

She is full of fascinating information of this kind. Another of her favourite hunting grounds is the Kensal Green cemetery – "a great tract of country in London" – hiding such delights as the grave of Blondin, the tightrope walker who walked over the Niagara Falls pushing his manager in a wheelbarrow – "the manager wanted to show that he had complete faith" – Trollope, Brunel and Thomas Hood – "they're all buried there". These ancient graves, long lost in undergrowth, are now being restored and improved. But they represent only the tip of the iceberg. There are thousands more secrets in the English countryside – "thousands upon thousands, billions and trillions more". Lucy Lambton wants "to give them the credit that's due to them, these wonderful things that are hidden away". She loves opening the eyes of others to their surroundings. "One of the best things ever was in a cinema in Slough when an old lady came up to me and said: 'I'd like you to know that I look at buildings now because of *you*.' She said no less. That was wonderful, wasn't it? I kissed her and kissed her. Wasn't it nice of her?"

The passion that preoccupied her at the time of the recording was her home – a Gothic rectory in Buckinghamshire. "I kiss its walls every day, I love it so much." A passion that preoccupies her all the time is food, particularly sweets. "If I have five pounds I'll spend it on a delicious bag of liquorice allsorts rather than keep it." Lucy Lambton totally rejects the idea that she is an upper-class dabbler, pottering around in the by-ways of the past. "At home I've got a word processor and a fax machine. I'm embroiled at the moment seventeen hours a day looking at modern architecture and being gripped by what's happening. The 'Sloane Ranger' label is a monstrously inaccurate one. It's just that I thunder on in my own life, which is ceaselessly entertaining and ceaselessly rewarding and very, very hard work and a joy."

Her great luxury would be to sit down with that word processor and record in detail all the things she has unearthed over the last thirty years. She could tell the story of Lord Kilmory who built an Egyptian mausoleum for his mistress in granite. Every time he moved house, the mausoleum moved with him, until, finally, he died and was buried in it in a gown of rats' fur alongside the woman he had loved; the funeral ceremony had already been rehearsed many times with him dressed in white and lying in a coffin pulled on wheels under the ground. These fascinating titbits are ready to pour, via the word processor, on to the page. They will arrive there embellished by love and excitement. Lucy Lambton never lets life get her down – "I get agonised by the hideous, dreadful horrors of the world – but if we're spotlighting this life we're talking about I don't get depressed about it."

So her luxury would be her word processor. Her book – a request more difficult to grant because it's a work of reference – was *The Dictionary of National Biography*. She beseeched me: "It's a work of glory," she implored. "Jeremy Bentham, the great law reformer, wrote a paper which I've found in it, saying that all altar icons should be made of the living dead. It says that Francis Bacon invented the deep freeze on Highgate Hill by freezing a chicken and then perishing of pneumonia and dying that night. It's so difficult to read it, too, because the words are the size of ants' legs – but it's a really wonderful book. I'm afraid I must insist."

I could not resist. Lucy Lambton should have her wish. Alone on her desert island she could feast even further on the curiosities of her country's past. But 'alone' is hardly the right word to describe a woman whose knowledge of such people as Lady Mount Edgcumbe, Lord Kilmory, Blondin the tightrope walker, Jeremy Bentham and Francis Bacon brings them alive. They'd be there, too – in spirit if not in the flesh – a little bemused, perhaps, but pleased to find themselves in such invigorating and intelligent company.

Lucinda Lambton

Impromptu in G flat Op. 90 No. 3 (Schubert)
Appenzeller (yodelling song)
Love Hurts – The Everly Brothers
A Four-legged Friend – Roy Rogers and Sons of the Pioneers
Quartet from *Fidelio* (Beethoven)
A Fool Such As I – Elvis Presley
Lost Lover Blues – Lottie Kimbrough
La Marseillaise

Book: *The Dictionary of National Biography*

Luxury: *A word processor*

LORD HAILSHAM

"I wish you'd hurry up and do the programme," said Lord Hailsham's secretary on the telephone, "he's driving us all mad marching round the house humming strange tunes." Lord Hailsham was my first castaway on *Desert Island Discs* and he entered into the experience with enthusiasm. He readily admits that he is not particularly musical but his choice of eight records was not only personal and lively but reflected, with great enjoyment, his long and busy life. When our researcher went to see him she found him struggling to remember a piece of music. "Can you help me?" he asked her and began to tum-te-tum vigorously. At last he stopped. "Any ideas?" he enquired. "Could it be," replied our researcher nervously, alarmed lest she should irritate His Lordship with a trivial response, "could it be 'I Do Like to Be Beside the Seaside'?"

"That's it!" cried Lord Hailsham, beaming with delight. "I knew you'd get it! Thank you so much!" Lord Hailsham may not be a great musician – but he knows exactly what he likes.

Quintin McGarel Hogg QC was born in 1907. In his lifetime he has been a scholar, a lawyer and a politician. He was once described as the cleverest boy to go to Eton and he ended his career by combining his political and legal abilities to become the longest-serving Chancellor this century. His father had held the post, too – a father-and-son record for which there are three historical precedents, but all of them "too ancient and too dubious" to count, says Lord Hailsham. The Woolsack is an important position, but not a particularly public one. In many people's minds I suspect he is best remembered as Quintin Hogg, the rumbustious Conservative politician, thrilling the faithful at many a Party conference with his oratory and his antics. Once he might have become their leader. Today he is one of their elder statesmen, a thoughtful, pure Conservative with a grandstand view of his party's recent history.

"A man who wants to be Prime Minister is a fool . . ."

To Lord Hailsham the prospect of being trapped on a desert island held few terrors. "I think I could manage – after a fashion." He could endure the loneliness but would miss his wife, he said. There were some things he would be quite happy to get away from – morning newspapers, for instance, "and the nonsense about 'rows' and 'furies' and 'bans' and 'crackdowns', and all the jargon of modern urban life".

Armed with these reflections he began to take me through his life, from his days in the family nursery before the First World War to the present time, when, in retirement, he "looks towards the end". His first choice was the one our researcher had identified for him: 'I Do Like to Be Beside the Seaside' sung by Mark Sheridan in a 1910 recording. It reminded him of the nursery and the old-fashioned gramophone kept there. It reminded him, too, of the song on the other side, 'Everybody's Doing It'. It was about a new dance called the Turkey Trot, which had come from America, a forerunner of the foxtrot.

"I think we know 'Everybody's Doing It'," I said. Lord Hailsham didn't seem impressed. "Everybody's doing it, doing it, doing it," he sang. "Everybody's doing it now!"

He then went on to paint a picture of an orthodox Edwardian childhood. He and his brother, Neil, would be in the nursery while his mother was downstairs "being very much more respectable". He remembered that sometimes they would be taken to have tea with their parents, or to be shown off after lunch. "We were fed on little lumps of crystalline coffee sugar, and all the mothers, cousins, aunts and sisters would be there, and my father would be presiding."

He didn't think that he was a particularly lovable child. "I think rather a horrid little boy in some ways – as arrogant as I subsequently became, though of course much smaller, and much more timid." He also confessed to being "intellectually precocious" although "morally rather the reverse", and had found a word to describe this early personality – "Hyperactive, I believe, is the modern phrase."

The bumptious and obviously rather naughty young Quintin Hogg had one guiding star – his mother. "She was exceedingly beautiful. She came from Tennessee, which is just on the border between the north and south in the United States. An old family, who'd been there since before the Revolution. She died suddenly, and to me, unexpectedly, when I was seventeen, and it was a great shock, a terrible shock. She was so vivacious that when my father first met her, in Bath, before he'd become engaged to her, he said she was at the far end of a room which was full of people, and somehow her influence had galvanised the whole assembly as if a spark of electricity had run across."

In 1920 he was sent off to Eton – as a scholarship boy. He was, he said, extremely happy there.

"The first days of Eton, of course, were a complete muddle. I was sent to the wrong room, and to the wrong schoolrooms, even the wrong chapel, of which there are two. But no, no, Eton is more like a university. It's a collection of houses, and I was in the best house of all, which was College." He was clever and he worked hard. I couldn't help wondering if he was a bit of a swot?

"They called it a 'sap' at Eton. But yes, I'm afraid I was a bit of a pot-hunter. I was very ambitious. I went after the prizes and I often got them. The only thing about it is that other boys there are as clever as you are, and can easily put you down, teach you a little bit of humility. Though in my case it was more difficult."

Lord Hailsham may dislike himself for being so conceited at such an early age – but it can't be denied that he had something to be conceited about. Unlike most schoolboys he loved his Latin and Greek. "They were marvellous, absolutely marvellous," he told me. "I wouldn't be without them now for the world, although they're rusty and old, and can only be drawn out of their scabbard with the greatest of difficulty, but they still mean an enormous lot to me."

He explained this love of the classics in terms that made him sound as much like a member of the Roman Senate as a modern parliamentarian.

"Well, European civilisation, whether you're reading French classical poetry, or whether you're reading almost anything, is deeply rooted in the past. The medieval church, and right back to the classical days of Marathon and Salamis and all the great natural virtues, like courage and integrity and patriotism. These things were part of the ideology of the ancient world. If we cut ourselves off from our roots, we are like cut flowers and ultimately we shall be withered and thrown away."

In those days, life for Lord Hailsham seemed to have a natural progression. After Eton came Oxford. He went there in 1926. But if, up until now, his life had seemed to follow an almost predestined course, it was while he was at university that something happened which was to change it for ever. His father was appointed Lord Chancellor and elevated to the peerage.

"The hereditary peerage was compulsory, you see. The original donee of the peerage might be a volunteer, but the eldest son was a conscript. And I don't like being conscripted."

For Hailsham this was an agonising moment. He was torn between love of his father and a desire to pursue a political career himself.

"I was devoted to my father, and he was absolutely shattered by the widowhood to which he had been subjected. Between him and Neville Chamberlain, was the choice of being Prime Minister. They were the two leading figures in the Conservative Party, and I realised that by taking the Lord Chancellorship, he was precluding his own succession to the throne."

Those were the feelings of a loving son. But what about those of an ambitious young man?

"I had been thinking, until that moment, in terms of a political career of the conventional kind: election to the House of Commons as a member of my party, representing a constituency, and perhaps taking office. If you are an hereditary peer, and you have to succeed, all the high offices of State, including the two Law Officerships, are debarred from you. But I wasn't so much upset because, to do me credit, I really was more concerned about my father. I thought he was a wonderful man, and history might have been different had he been chosen instead of Neville Chamberlain, who knows?"

History, I reminded him, might have been different nearly thirty years later had Hailsham been chosen as leader of the Conservative Party instead of Sir Alec Douglas-Home. He did not disagree. "It would have been," he announced firmly.

Quintin Hogg was forty-three when he succeeded his father to the peerage. He made it plain in all quarters, including to the Prime Minister, that he wanted to disclaim the title, but it was thirteen years before legislation was put in place which enabled him to do so. Even then it was a close-run thing. A single vote prevented the new law applying only to those peers who had never taken their seat.

Lord Hailsham described to me how his interest in politics began. He lived in a family which had for many years been involved in public life and the law: "My father instructed me in some of the more subtle doctrines of Common Law. Even when I was in the nursery, he'd come and say goodnight to us, and talk to us about his cases, and he'd explain to me all about the law of libel and slander, and breach of warranty, and fraud, and he'd tell me about the Money Lenders' Act, so that it was a natural thing for me to take on the colour of my father."

I wondered if Quintin Hogg, the classics student, had nursed a desire to become Prime Minister. "I don't think one does want to be Prime Minister. I think a man who wants to be Prime Minister is a fool. But a man who enters a profession likes to do well in it, and if all the major prizes are cut off from you, if I may coin a phrase 'at a stroke', I think you do feel a little browned off."

Hailsham, however, accepted his lot. He left Oxford, was called to the Bar and practised successfully as a lawyer. Then, in the late thirties, his father suffered a stroke. Suddenly Hailsham found that his political ambitions had been rekindled. He told his father that if he was to be an hereditary peer he wanted to do the job properly and gain an apprenticeship in the House of Commons. He was rewarded by being placed on the Conservative Party's approved list of candidates.

"I hawked myself round every constituency I could find. Nobody was at all interested – at all. And then, in 1938, I was right up in the Scottish Highlands with an old friend called Alex Bell, and the news came through one Sunday evening on the steam radio, that poor Bobbie Bourne, who had been the member for Oxford, had gone to church that morning and died walking home with his family. And Alex said to me, 'Why don't you go in for Oxford?' And I said, 'Don't be silly, we're fifteen miles from the nearest post office and they are not interested in any case.' He said, 'If you will send a telegram, I will see that it gets there tomorrow morning.' I did, and the next thing I knew I was selected as the candidate."

Lord Hailsham believes that the by-election he fought was the most spectacular of the inter-war period. It took place not long after Munich and ended up as a two-horse race between Hailsham and the Master of Balliol who had been brought in at the last moment to replace both the Labour and Liberal candidates.

"And so Munich, the Master of Balliol and this untried Conservative candidate, entered into the lists of the first by-election after Munich. And from that moment I was famous."

Hailsham had believed in the Munich agreement and in Chamberlain. I put it to him that he was what was known as an appeaser.

"I wasn't an appeaser. I did believe in Munich, and I do believe that we wouldn't have won the war without it. It was a trip wire. The country could not have gone into war divided, and it was divided in 1938. But even more important, the gun fighters, which won the Battle of Britain – the Hurricanes and Spitfires – were not in service. We'd have fought with Furies, and we'd have been beaten."

Not long after that, politics were forgotten as the war began in earnest. It was 1940 and Quintin Hogg, now thirty-three, was posted to the Middle East. He went to say goodbye to his father.

"We sat in the Carlton Club when it was being bombed. A great big bomb burst through the roof, and over our heads. I had to carry my father out of the Carlton Club, because by that time he was paralysed all down one side. And I thought to myself as I saw the sky through the roof: This is just like Aeneas carrying Anchises out of the ruins of Troy."

After that our conversation turned to other family matters – his long and happy marriage to his wife, Mary. The couple married in 1944 and had five children. He gave the impression, I told him, that women had been very important in his life.

"I think they have," he replied, "I'm a natural man, and I must say I enjoy female company."

It was in 1978 that Lord Hailsham's first wife was killed in a riding accident in Australia. They had been together for thirty-four years.

"It was a terrible shock. She was twelve years younger than me. We were as happy as on our honeymoon during that visit to Australia. We were enjoying ourselves. We were riding around something rather bigger than Rotten Row in a thing called the Centennial Park in Sydney. The horse ran away with her and must have shied at a bollard of some kind. It threw her over its right shoulder, I think. The next thing I saw she was lying there in a pool of blood, with her head broken in."

Lord Hailsham has always had a strong Christian faith. Although tested to the utmost, it remained resilient.

"My faith was not shaken, but the sun didn't shine any more in the day, and the birds didn't sing. I was a pelican in the wilderness, and the pelican is a water bird. And I was a sparrow on the rooftops, and the sparrow is a gregarious bird, and I was an owl, which is a woodland bird, and the flowers didn't bloom."

Suddenly the studio felt very quiet. It was obvious that this had been a devastating moment in Hailsham's life. The memory of it moved him deeply. But the riding accident had happened ten years previously and since then he has remarried. So, gently, I asked him, "But the sun shines again now?"

"The sun shines, yes," he replied. "But one carries scars of previous wounds with one, to one's dying day."

His next record was the hymn 'St Patrick's Breastplate' which was one of the first Lady Hailsham's favourites and was played at her funeral. That's the beauty of a programme like *Desert Island Discs*. It can allow for a moment of tender reflection and then, once the music is over, start again at a different pace and in a different mood.

We then returned to the hurly-burly of politics and the plotting and planning that went into finding a successor to Harold Macmillan. I told Lord Hailsham that I recalled him ringing that enormous handbell at a Conservative Party Conference and, on another occasion, entertaining press and public in baggy bathing trunks on Brighton beach. He had been an adept publicist for the Tory Party, quite a showman, I suggested.

"It wasn't that I was a showman. After Suez, the party had fallen into very low morale. Harold, the Prime Minister, was busy being Prime Minister. His way of looking at things was to play it down, play it long, and play it cool. Well we weren't going to win the 1959 election by playing it down, playing it long, playing it cool. That might be the way to be Prime Minister, but it wasn't the way to encourage the faithful. And, therefore, studying Harold, I did the opposite, being, as I believe I was, a good advocate. The whole of a barrister's life is devoted, (a) to concealing his own identity, and (b) to sacrificing himself for his client."

Nevertheless, hadn't he thoroughly enjoyed it all at the same time?

"Well, one doesn't do a thing unless one enjoys it – at least one doesn't do it well unless one enjoys it – and I threw myself into my job."

His enthusiasm was interpreted in some quarters as an attempt to upstage the Prime Minister, but if Harold Macmillan didn't approve, Hailsham wasn't aware of it.

"I saw no sign of that at all. I think he was a little startled, because he didn't know what he'd bought. It was Oliver Poole who made me Party Chairman, or rather Harold did on Oliver Poole's suggestion. Oliver Poole knew exactly what he was up to."

Whatever the circumstances, Hailsham had become enormously popular. I moved us on to the time when, he has always said, Harold Macmillan told him that he wanted him to be the next Prime Minister. It was 1963.

"When he sent for me on the Monday, telling me that he was going and he wanted me to succeed him, neither he knew at that moment, nor did I, that two days later he'd be taken in for an emergency operation and actually have his prostate removed. It was during that week that all this sort of business took place."

It's one of the fascinating questions of Britain's post-war politics: what went wrong?

"Well, to begin with, I think there were people in the party who would have preferred Rab Butler, I think very reasonably. There were people in the party who thought, unreasonably, that I was too far to the right for their liking. There's always been a tendency in the Conservative Party to play safe if you can, which is a very dangerous thing to do. One should take a calculated risk if one has to. They said how marvellous it would be if only Alec would consent, and that's exactly what happened. Macmillan advised the Queen to send for Alec, and we all served happily under him."

The change in his fortunes did not disappoint him. "I was very distressed at the way in which I'd been traduced by people whom I had helped to get into power. There were people who'd spread hideous stories about me, and I was very much distressed. But disappointed at not being Prime Minister? No, never."

I came back to his earlier point – how different would history have been if he had succeeded to the premiership in 1963? "Like the White Knight: I don't say it would be better, I only say it would have been different." And then, with a grin: "I think we'd have won the 1964 election."

However, that failure to become Prime Minister and the election defeat of 1964 gradually steered Hailsham away from mainstream party politics. He had renounced his title in order to continue as an MP, but, with the Tories now out of office, he returned to the Bar. When they returned to power in 1970, he accepted a life peerage and served, as Lord Chancellor, in both Edward Heath's and Margaret Thatcher's governments. To end our conversation I asked him about the changes he'd seen in the Party. What had been its greatest loss and what its greatest gain?

"I believe in the two-party system. I don't believe in more major parties than two, and I don't believe in one, because one will either break up or cause a tyranny. An elective dictatorship, I think is the phrase I once used. Now the Conservative Party is the party by nature which challenges the spirit of the age in the light of the traditions of the past. It says to the Liberal of the nineteenth century, 'Look, making money isn't everything. There is law. There is welfare.' It says to the socialist, who is the paternalist, 'Look, there is freedom. There is movement. There is variety.' Now this has put us, in recent years, in a very strange position."

Hailsham believes that Macmillan wanted to create a Conservative Party that could defend a system which embraced both private enterprise and public ownership. He thought, says Hailsham, that Gaitskell would win his battle to soften the more extreme aspects of Labour Party socialism. But it became obvious that what Hailsham calls "the ratchet effect of socialism in the Labour Party" was such that there would always be a tide which, in his view, had to be turned.

"This is what Margaret Thatcher has succeeded in doing. She's changed the face of British politics. But, of course, the price has been that the Conservative Party, which is by nature the party of criticism, and wisdom and quiet, has become the *radical* party, and it is the Labour Party which is now conservative, clinging pathetically to its old fallacies. Now this is a reversal of rôles, and it is a very remarkable thing to have happened. It's been all to the good, I think, except that sooner or later a new radical party must emerge to take the part and place of the Labour Party. The great mistake is to think it could be a party of the centre. The British constitution depends upon the politics of effective choice, and I am waiting to see how the rôles will be recaptured."

Of the seven Prime Ministers under whom he had served, or whom he had supported, which did he think would go down in history as the greatest?

"I don't think it's possible, so close to them, to make a judgement on that. I think Churchill stands obviously in a class by himself. He happened to have been born, and to have matured, at exactly the time when history required such a curiously shaped piece on the board, and he was a man of genius. Cardinal Newman used to say that he looked in vain for the finger of God in history. He said it was like looking into a mirror, expecting to see his own face and seeing nothing. Now the one case in which I think I can see the finger of God in contemporary history, is Churchill's arrival at that precise moment in 1940."

With this observation, our discussion drew to a close. But not before telling me that retirement was "absolute hell". It was, he said, "like being withdrawn from addictive drugs and being made to play a game of football at the same time". I asked for his promise that the bathtub he chose as his luxury would not be turned upside down so that he could shelter beneath it.

"I will make that promise," said Lord Hailsham, indulging in a last classical flourish. "I am no Diogenes."

Lord Hailsham

I Do Like to Be Beside the Seaside – Mark Sheridan
Swing Low Sweet Chariot – Paul Robeson
Dancing on the Ceiling – Jessie Mathews
'O frag mich nicht' from *The Faithful Peasant* (Fall) – Fritz Wunderlich
Regimental March of the Rifle Brigade
St Patrick's Breastplate (I Bind unto Myself Today)
'Vivat Regina' section from *I Was Glad* (Parry) from the
Coronation of Queen Elizabeth II
Dies irae (Gregorian chant)

Book: *Works of Homer*

Luxury: *A bathtub and soap*

THORA HIRD

It's difficult to know where Thora Hird, actress, ends and Thora Hird, person, begins. That, of course, is her secret. Throughout the recording of the programme she would munch a biscuit or clink her coffee cup, each time apologising for the acoustic diversion she had caused. Was she just being her natural, chatty self? Or did she know that such endearing behaviour was what her audience would expect from her? It doesn't matter. The fact is that we felt compelled to leave at least one of her interruptions in the final version – simply because it was so delightful – and that her interview received the highest Appreciation Index of any *Desert Island Discs* which I've presented. People love Thora. They respond to her warmth and ease of manner. She told me that if she hadn't become an actress she would have liked to run a little corner shop selling all sorts of useful items such as mothballs. I believe her – and I can see her in my mind's eye attracting the same sort of fascinated attention from behind her counter as she does on the stage or the screen.

Thora Hird's naturalness and her happiness to talk about her life in an unfettered way didn't make her an easy person to interview. She talks a great deal. She's very bubbly – and enjoys shooting off at a tangent. My task was to keep her on the subject without cramping her style. Together we made it.

"You know me well enough to know I've no swank."

Thora Hird is one of those people who sets you tingling with pleasure. It's not just that she's warm and professional. There's a tremendous certainty about her, too: she approaches everything with a robustness and clarity that's very refreshing. She's had a fascinating life, and it's never thrown her. Whether touring in rep in the north of England, working at Ealing Film Studios before the war, mastering a part in an Alan Bennett play or presenting a religious programme on television, she remains inescapably herself. Like all great performers, her ability to do many things is built upon her naturally attractive qualities. Whoever she plays, whatever she does, she's always Thora Hird.

We started the programme by remembering the only acting part she says she got through influence. Her mother was in a play that was being produced by her father. Thora Hird played her baby. She was eight weeks old. "My mother was playing the village maid who had been done wrong by the squire's son, so I suppose I played the unfortunate result. My dad was about forty years ahead in the business – and he wouldn't have a baby with a wooden head in a shawl that might knock against the scenery. So he said to my mother, 'Take her on'." And on she went, beginning a career that has lasted as long as she has lived.

Thora Hird was born and brought up in Morecambe in Lancashire. Her mother was a singer called Marie Mare, her father, James Henry Hird, doubled up as front-of-house manager and comedian. Thora remembers that her mother always said that Mr Hird proposed to his future wife at a time when she was being pursued by a stage-door Johnny. "The Johnnies used to wait at the stage door for the girls with flowers, and one Johnny waited about four nights. The next day my mum and dad went on a picnic and he proposed that day just in case the fellow was there again that night." The couple toured everywhere – "they boasted they had been in every county in England and had postcards to prove it" – but eventually came back to Mrs Hird's home town of Morecambe. It wasn't easy to get a job, so Thora's father earned his living running a swimming pool at the end of the promenade. "He was everything in charge," said Thora – but soon he got promotion. "He went as manager on the West End pier and then after that to the Alhambra, and then after the Alhambra to the Royalty Theatre, and from the Royalty Theatre to the Central Pier." This progression through the hierarchy of Morecambe's theatreland meant that for his daughter, too, the stage became a way of life. He taught her everything she knew.

"He was very critical – but always constructive. If I do know anything about comedy timing or pathos – anything – I owe it to my dad. Nothing was too much trouble." He would coach her all the time, even when the family were eating, teaching his daughter among other things where to put the inflection on a word. "It's extraordinary," she said, "how if you just put the inflection on one word and not another, it's a funny line."

Thora Hird went to a private school – "one-and-six a week, very posh" – which she loved. But Thora was due to leave at the end of the term in which she would be fourteen. "The day they were all going back to school I put a clean blouse and gymslip on and I stood in the front-room window at home. And my mother said: 'Thora, where are you?' I was watching the girls go up our street to school. Our mother never said a word. She just got my schoolbag, brought it in, put it on the table and said: 'Go and ask Miss Nelson if you can go back for another term.' I was out quicker than I've told you. And I've never sung 'Holy, holy, holy' so well in my life as that morning when I went back to school. I loved it."

Although born and bred for the theatre, Thora first appeared in amateur productions directed by her father, in one of which she met "the best waltzer *ever*" – and then repeated it, "*ever!*" He was called Freddy Tomlinson and "Oh, he was a good waltzer. I've waltzed reverse, no trouble. Ooh, our Fred!" She remembered how she had seen Jessie Matthews in a film at the local cinema wearing a dress that was half black velvet and half silver lurex. Thora went "four times in the ninepennies to draw it and then went to the little lady round the corner, Mrs Harewood, who made it for me. And I can remember the first time I wore that dress, waltzing with Freddy Tomlinson and thinking, just excuse me, would you: look at this!"

It was a lovely story, full of fun and humour, evoking a world that's now disappeared for ever. Thora Hird's memories of those days are very strong and remain an important part of her. For instance, after leaving school she worked for a while at the local Co-op, where she observed the customers whom she would one day use as the basis for characters. "I think I've played them nearly all. When I'm not a good enough actress to build a character, I'll think of somebody that came in the Co-op. I think – put a bit of Mrs X in there." And not only customers get used in this way, but relatives too. Thora Hird has a certain voice – "the well-off voice" she calls it – which relies heavily on her auntie from Manchester. She told me this story too.

"When I was about five or six, I was in Manchester, and she gave me some watercress for my tea. The shop bell went, and she went through the curtain saying" (and here Thora put on a gruff northern voice) "'Eat that.' But when she got into the shop, I heard her say" (and here came Thora's refined voice) "'Oh, hello Mrs Armitage.' Being little, I thought you had to have a voice in a shop that was different to the one you had when you were feeding somebody with watercress."

In 1931, when she was twenty years old, Thora Hird began her full career. She'd appeared in rep a few times, being paid a pound a week, but not playing many important parts. In one – a play called *As You Are* – she was cast as the mother-in-law and George Formby came to see it because Ealing Studios were to make it into a film with him as the star. Formby was so taken with Thora's performance that he asked her if she'd like to play the same rôle in the film. "Can you imagine?" she asked me. "A pound a week in rep and somebody said: 'I'd love you to play it in the film.' I mean, this was unattainable." A few days later a casting director came to see her. "He said: 'I have come from London to see you play.' And I said: 'Oh, but the fare's £3 17s 9d' – it was then, to London – and he said, 'Well never mind that, we may go out to supper.' And I have to tell you we did. But all I had was a Horlicks because I couldn't eat anything." This touching tale doesn't have a perfect fairytale ending, however. In the end, Thora wasn't given the part. But she did get a contract – "ten pounds a week if I didn't work, ten pounds a day if I did". Her life as a full-time actress had begun.

Her first film was *Black Sheep of Whitehall* starring Will Hay. Interestingly enough, it was the real Thora Hird, rather than her screen test, which landed her the part. She had been given a beauty treatment for the test – lashes, curls, rosebud lips and all – but when it came to the shoot her inexperience caused her to cry out halfway through: "Well, that's it. If I haven't done it right now there's no point in it. I didn't ask to come down. You asked me." When he eventually saw the test, Will Hay ignored the curls, the lashes and the lips and merely concentrated on her outburst. "What a face!" he said. "Send her a telegram." And Thora won her first part – for being Thora. Because, as she herself admitted: "I've never been a raving beauty, you see."

Thora Hird's first West End theatre appearance was at the Vaudeville in 1944, playing Mrs Game in *No Medals* with Fay Compton and Frederick Leister. She then appeared as Mrs Holmes in *Flowers for the Living* – a play which, she says, "did everything for me". It's said to have been her favourite part but Thora Hird couldn't quite claim it as that. "Not my *favourite* part," she said. "But a very, very good part – a heartbreaking part – and the following day there were so many offers for films and things." She couldn't do them all but remembered the lovely feeling it gave her. As well as West End theatre she's also played classical rôles. For BBC Television she appeared as the nurse in *Romeo and Juliet* and Mrs Hardcastle in *She Stoops to Conquer*. But all these performances, important though they were, acted as a background to the work which, more than any other, has brought her acclaim today and introduced her to a wider audience. This is her collaboration with Alan Bennett and particularly her portrayal of Doris in *A Cream Cracker Under the Settee* for which she was given the 1989

British Academy of Film and Television Arts award for best actress. Thora, typically, gives more credit to the writer than she does to herself.

"This is clever Alan, this is Alan Bennett, Mr Wonder-man. Alan can write a line which said one way would break your heart; said another way it is very, very funny. But to me, the one thing that strikes me about Alan is that he writes so well that he doesn't have to mention a word. Everybody didn't see *Cream Cracker*, but in it I mention my baby, saying I would have liked to have called it John but the nurse said it wasn't fit to be called anything, lying there in the newspaper. Alan might just as well have put over the screen 'Miscarriage, miscarriage'. You knew."

Of her own performance she remains more critical. "I would never see myself thinking: Thor, that's it. Ten out of ten." But she did feel moved, she told me, when she saw a recording of it, adding: "I was fighting not to be moved when I was playing it too, I'll tell you."

She admires Bennett for his wit as well and recounted one of her favourite scenes in a play where she was a patient in a hospital. A little Japanese boy brings in a box of chocolates for someone and offers one to the character she is playing. At which the character remarks: "It'll take more than a box of Cadbury's Milk Tray to wipe out the memory of Pearl Harbor." It's a terrific line, and as she told it to me sitting across the table in the studio I could conjure up the scene instantly, and the look on Thora Hird's face. That's the point about an actress like her. The line is very strong: it's naturally funny. But Thora Hird's face and her voice, with all those inflections taught to her by her father years ago in Morecambe, capture the speech and deliver it safely to the audience. Very often it reaches them in better condition than when it left the author's pen.

To a large number of television viewers, Thora Hird is known as the presenter of the religious programme *Praise Be*, now more than twelve years old. She herself has very strong religious convictions – "I couldn't do without my pal upstairs," she told me, "I couldn't," and her love of God, combined with her friendly, easy approach, have made this a programme to which people write in their thousands. "It's amazing the pleasure it gives people. I never realised there were so many people in the world with *no one* – not even a fourth cousin removed – so many people alone." She is proud that people who watch her feel that she is in the room with them, glad that it's something she is able to give them. She's anxious that this genuine pleasure is not interpreted as conceit. There's no fear of that. As she herself says: "You know me well enough to know I've no swank." Her enjoyment at giving a little bit of herself in this way comes from the fact that she is very content in her own life. She's been happily married to her husband, Scottie, for fifty years. She's proud of her daughter, the actress Janette Scott, and her "lovely" son-in-law and two healthy grandchildren. "I've so much love around me that it is easy for me to give a bit out." Her happiness is religious as well as domestic. "I say my prayers to the Lord walking about the house many-a-time," she said.

Her last record was 'Onward Christian Soldiers'. "I could march about the island with this," she said. "I love it. All my life I've loved this hymn. I wouldn't mind them playing it when I've had it, if you want to know." The book she wanted to take was her own, called *Scene and Hird*. "There's no conceit in this," she explained. "There's so much of my childhood in it and I might forget a bit on the island – so I'd take that to have a read and remind myself." Her luxury was "a nice bit of cleansing milk. I'm not going to bother with all the washing lark. I might have a swim. But a little bit of cleansing milk would be nice. And some tissues. You know – the little outfit."

Her little outfit granted without demur, Thora Hird could now look forward to life on the radio island. Although she wouldn't enjoy it very much – "I'm not very fond of my own company," she had told me at the outset of the programme – I felt sure that she would keep herself busy. She's a great cleaner-upper. "I'm nearly a nuisance," she confessed. "I don't mean that disease about getting up and cleaning the house, then starting again. But I'm a little bit tidy, if I may say." When she wasn't being busy she'd have those marvellous childhood memories to sustain her – Morecambe in its heyday and the world of variety and theatre. She had told me one story about four cousins of hers who'd taught her to tap-dance when she was very young – "walloping" they called it – and I could imagine Thora sitting in her deckchair absorbed in her book and idly tapping her foot as the memory of those infant lessons came back into her mind. Would she, I wonder, in the privacy of her own island ever dare to try out the dance steps again? Or would she prefer to recite the lines from a favourite play? I never asked.

It doesn't matter, because without an audience there can never be a real performance. But I hope the dumb inhabitants of Thora's new domain, whether flesh, fish or fowl, will realise what a talent has come among them and how missed it is at home.

Thora Hird

Temptation Rag – Pasadena Roof Orchestra
Blaze Away – Royal Artillery Band
Gold and Silver Waltz (Lehár) – Johann Strauss Orchestra of Vienna
Cumberland Gap – Lonnie Donegan
None but the Lonely Heart (Tchaikovsky)
When the Saints Go Marching In
Andante from Piano Concerto No. 21 (Mozart) – Richard Clayderman
Onward Christian Soldiers

Book: *Scene and Hird* (Thora Hird)

Luxury: *Cleansing milk*

JEFFREY TATE

Not having met Jeffrey Tate before I didn't quite know what to expect. He turned out to be delightfully easy and articulate, an ideal 'castaway' whose interesting life was matched by supreme musical taste. He gave the impression of a man who enjoys life – not because he has overcome a crippling disability to do so, but because his feelings and appetites lead him naturally towards good things.

I had been interviewed myself by a national newspaper on the day we recorded Jeffrey Tate's programme for *Desert Island Discs*. Perhaps that made me more sensitive than usual to the rigours of being questioned. Certainly there was something in the air that afternoon – something which produced a programme I still remember for its delicacy.

Jeffrey Tate's robustness could not disguise his deep feelings. Among his records was Billie Holliday's 'I'll Be Seeing You' and he insisted that we changed the running order so it could be played at the end. When he listened to it during the recording there were tears in his eyes. The memories it evoked had touched him deeply. He didn't mind that it showed, just as he didn't mind speaking frankly. Being sensitive does not prevent one from being tough, and I thought I detected both characteristics in Jeffrey Tate.

"I would like to have been born in the thirties as a cabaret pianist."

In his childhood, Jeffrey Tate's friends were musical notes rather than other children. He is an instinctive musician. Although his mother played the piano rather well and his grandfather, a Welshman, introduced him to the rudiments of opera, his own talent grew from within. When his parents wanted him to stop piano lessons "to concentrate on more important things", he just carried on. His great childhood love was to take a book, put it on the piano and improvise as he was reading, creating the mood of the book at the keyboard. "I would sit for hours playing. I was perfectly happy then and would not miss anybody," he says.

Music as a friend, as a companion, was one of the dominant themes of my interview with Jeffrey Tate. All his records had been chosen in an attempt to create an environment in which "I won't be too lonely". But it was an environment that was far from solemn or serious. His music was full of love, and nostalgia too. There was a carol from King's College, Cambridge, and Noël Coward singing 'Poor Little Rich Girl'. If he had his life again, he said, he would "like to have been born in the thirties as a cabaret pianist", and to prove it he sang a rather good impersonation of Noël Coward in full voice. He's a great admirer of Coward – "that timing, and that wit, and that sadness underneath meant an awful lot to me when I was young".

Jeffrey Tate cannot stand in front of an orchestra like most other conductors. His disability means that he has to perch on a high stool, but it's not a situation which he finds limiting or frustrating. "What I used to think would happen," he said, "is that I'd get physically tired of holding my hands up in the air, and doing it over great spans of time." But on his fortieth birthday he gave himself a treat and conducted *Parsifal* for nearly six hours.

"When I finished it, I felt I could have conducted bits of it again. So after that I thought there is actually, in the last resort, no limit to my own physical energy – if I really know what I'm doing and want to be doing it. I then gave up any of the worry about it being too exhausting for me."

Even so, the position in which he finds himself must at times make him very self-conscious. I asked him how he managed the problem of getting to the podium in the first place. How did he feel as he walked on in front of an audience? He confessed that he did feel a bit odd. But he has taught himself to do it slowly – after one night in Cologne when his entrance ended in disaster.

"I rushed on to the podium, well, I was going to rush on to the podium, when I slipped on the first step, and fell into the arms of the viola player.

It took me about half an hour to recover from that, and I had to conduct. I learned a savage lesson: I really have to, despite feeling nervous and very self-conscious, walk very, very slowly. I force myself to do that now."

The disability from which Jeffrey Tate suffers is curvature of the spine. But it wasn't spotted at first when he was very young. His parents thought he had flat feet, but as he got older it became clear that he had something more serious. After a week's observation in hospital it emerged that the young Jeffrey had a complex set of diseases which amounted to a combination of double curvature of the spine and spina bifida. As a result, at the age of eight he spent six months in hospital for one big operation and then, when he was twelve, two months for another. In between were all the "perpetual check-ups and terrible visits to places which had to measure surgical shoes for me. I got fed up with it. It was just very boring."

One of my other guests who features in this book, Gerald Scarfe, was also plagued by childhood illness. I was struck by the fact that in both cases, although doctors and parents had undoubtedly done their best for them, it was the children's stoicism and determination which had had the greatest beneficial effect. Gerald Scarfe was given cures for asthma, but in the end it was his own self-reliance which drove the illness away. Jeffrey Tate was given physical contraptions which he had to have the courage to abandon. He had a leg iron for a while – but it didn't work and was cast aside. One day, he finally abandoned everything. He had been given a plastic brace which he wore religiously from the age of twelve until he was in his thirties. "It was a horrible thing. It had holes in it and it started just below my arms and went to my groin." One hot summer's day, when he was in France, he decided he could wear it no more. "I took the damn thing off and went back to my surgeon and said, 'Look!'" The surgeon accepted his patient's liberation calmly. He has never worn it again.

Ill children often have fewer opportunities to make friends. "When I went into hospital for the first time, I felt profoundly lonely and worried because I didn't like being in hospital. It's funny how an atmosphere of children all on their own isn't a particularly happy one – *Lord of the Flies* is not an unreasonable book in that sense. Children are very nasty to each other, particularly in isolation, and under stress. I learned to lie and do all sorts of terrible things that I hadn't really done before. Then afterwards, as the disability got worse, I began to look different, and couldn't take part in activities, and I did feel isolated. On the other hand, I did realise that my brain, thank God, wasn't affected."

He was lucky in that his school, Farnham Grammar, was not frightened of encouraging a boy in his condition. The school was, he says, "immensely sympathetic in all respects", to the extent that the headmaster – "who dared a lot" – made Jeffrey Tate head boy. But did he ever worry, when accolades of this kind were bestowed on him, that this might simply be out of sympathy? His answer was candid: "I often think I'm getting a sympathy vote. I have to be convinced that what I'm doing is because I'm worth it and not because people are saying, 'Well, you know, it's rather amazing that he's doing it' – I still suffer from that. I don't think I shall ever lose it. It's something that's built into having a disability, and it's there."

A youth overshadowed by hospital visits and painful operations led Jeffrey Tate to think of medicine as a career, because he felt "a great sense of debt". He felt that he'd learned to walk and stay mobile because of what medicine had done for him. His parents encouraged him in this too. They wanted him to have a stable career, one in which his disability would be protected to a certain extent, rather than one in the more chancy world of the arts. But try though he might, Jeffrey Tate could not let medicine win the battle over music. He failed his exams first time around. Not deliberately, but because at St Thomas's in London, where he'd gone after Cambridge, the attractions of opera workshop lured him away from his hospital duties.

"I spent much more time coaching Rhine maidens than walking the wards," he says. They obviously had a similar effect on the young Jeffrey as they had had on the sailors of German legend. It wasn't long before he was completely off course, working at both opera and medicine in equal amounts. The inevitable happened: he finally passed his exams and won a place at the London Opera Centre at the same time. He opted for opera, on the understanding that he could always go back to medicine if he wanted. It has never reclaimed him.

For seven years, from 1970 to 1976, Jeffrey Tate was a repetiteur at Covent Garden – "bashing notes into singers – it's the dogsbody of an opera house, and great fun". He was very happy and entertained no thoughts of doing much else. Much in demand, he enjoyed his reputation as a sympathetic and intelligent coach. He worked with many famous singers, including Callas.

"It was the year before she died and she had been in isolation for a long time. She was very suspicious of me at first, as I was of her, but after the month was up I think we'd become really close friends. Whether I actually could coach her is another matter. I could occasionally, if she was in the right sort of mood, but it was difficult. She was an extraordinary person to be with – frightening on one level."

His break as a conductor came out of the blue. He had been assisting Pierre Boulez with his famous production of *The Ring* at Bayreuth when the offer came to conduct a production of *Carmen* at the Gothenburg opera. He was slightly reluctant about the move. He still is, as I found when I asked him if this experience had led him to the discovery of what he really wanted to do.

"No," he said, "that sounds very romantic and it wasn't at all. I still am not certain. I still don't know really what I ought to be doing in my life. I don't think I'll ever really know – I'm that sort of person. I still have my grave doubts about it. Maybe because conducting the music was the second thing in my life – maybe I have got the sort of Zigeuner wanderlust inside me and will never actually feel that I am at home in any one thing."

Curiously, Jeffrey Tate was not always an opera fan. "I loathed it for a long time. I used to go to Covent Garden and wonder why the singers were never with the beat and always sang out of tune. And why the productions looked so horrible. I would much rather go to the Royal Shakespeare Company." There are times when he still feels like that. But, in the end, as it won over medicine, so opera wins over the theatre too. "When it works, it is the most wonderful thing in the world."

We talked next about the art of conducting. Jeffrey Tate is sometimes criticised for taking classical music at too slow a pace, but he defends this. "I believe that music needs the time for all the details that are there to be made apparent and to be heard. I'm very keen that one should hear as many strands of the orchestra as possible." With orchestral players he uses his hands to explain what he wants, with singers he uses talk. "It all comes from the word in the last resort. The way you sing the notes themselves depends on the meaning of what you are singing. So I try and talk about meaning – and I try to do it via love. That is to say, to do it positively. I can never do anything by shouting at anybody. I have to seduce them into wanting to do it my way."

This gentle approach, and the use of the word 'love', suggested to me that Jeffrey Tate was a man who had come to terms with life and, despite his disability, found great peace. So presumably, he felt little bitterness these days about the fact that he had been crippled? His answer surprised me.

"Of course I'm bitter. I'd be stupid not to be bitter. There are times when I would love to be perfectly straight and perfectly normal and there are many occasions in my life in which it would have helped a great deal – others in which it wouldn't. The bitterness is part of a great sort of panoply. It's a useful thing to know about, bitterness, you know. I don't think it's bad to know what bitterness means. I'm not basically bitter, but it does perhaps represent seven to eight per cent of my life. Why not?"

Again, it was a candid answer – and, thinking about it, the answer of a man who was well-rounded and capable of coming to terms with difficulty. By accepting an element of bitterness he had absorbed it. It was a natural part of his life. Like his music, it belonged to him.

He confessed, rather shyly I thought, to two ambitions – one, "awfully arrogant", to conduct *The Ring* at Bayreuth, the other "which might happen", to conduct *Die Meistersinger* – "somewhere". When I advanced a third, he recoiled. What about running the Royal Opera House?

"That's a bit under the belt," he said, but then confessed, "If one day they wanted me to do it, I would perhaps love to. I might even be interested in administration."

Although he admits to an "interior fear" before a big performance, Jeffrey Tate felt that he was resourceful enough to cope on a desert island. He thought that I would never let him take a Meissen cup and saucer but would insist that he made a suitable receptacle himself out of the natural resources on the island. This, I felt, was a rather harsh judgement on *me*. After all, Meissen porcelain does possess qualities other than pure usefulness! But we compromised – and stole Piero della Francesca's *Nativity* from the National Gallery. (It could hang on the palm tree next to Arthur Scargill's *Mona Lisa*, I thought later.) He was allowed all the novels of Jane Austen (in one volume) because, as he said, "they're all nice and short".

Thus equipped, he was ready for his desert island stay. He would make himself comfortable, he had an elegant book, and a beautiful painting of people singing. His natural sense of nostalgia would feed his reflections while his talents as a musician occupied his emotions and his intellect. In many ways, a less disabled castaway it would be difficult to find.

Jeffrey Tate

Poor Little Rich Girl – Noël Coward

'Villes' from *Les Illuminations* (Britten) – Peter Pears

In the Bleak Mid-winter – Choir of King's College, Cambridge

The Banks of Green Willow (Butterworth) – English Chamber Orchestra conducted by Jeffrey Tate

'Quintet' from *Così fan tutte* (Mozart)

Symphony No. 104, 'London' (Haydn)

'Fliedermonolog' from *The Mastersingers of Nuremberg* (Wagner)

I'll Be Seeing You – Billie Holiday

Book: *Collected works of Jane Austen*

Luxury: *Piero della Francesca's painting of the Nativity*

NEIL KINNOCK

When I took over as presenter of *Desert Island Discs* I had the feeling that not many of our prominent politicians had appeared on the programme. I was anxious to correct this – but I had to be careful. My background in news and journalism meant that the audience might be alarmed if they were suddenly fed an unexpected and concentrated diet of parliamentary heavyweights. They might begin to imagine that the programme was being taken over by alien forces. As it was, I think in our first two years we managed a strong selection of long-serving MPs: Enoch Powell, Edward Heath, David Owen, Roy Jenkins, Lord Hailsham, Dennis Skinner, Ian Paisley, Douglas Hurd, Michael Foot, Tony Benn and Nigel Lawson. But I don't think anyone could say that they have dominated.

Politicians talking about themselves rather than their policies are always interesting. They tend to relax more. The 'hard sell' disappears, leaving behind a softer tone. So it was with Neil Kinnock. He's a man who uses his formidable eloquence at its best when he's talking about his roots – and I was pleased that he felt able to be as open as he was. As an occasion the recording was fairly unremarkable, but as a glimpse of an important public figure taking things at a gentler pace, it was revealing. I remember that he had great difficulty making up his mind about his luxury. He must have changed his choice about a dozen times. First he wanted a guitar with an endless supply of strings, then he changed to shaving gear, then he plumped for a shoe-cleaning kit – and finally decided on something altogether different.

Neil Kinnock is a man who, until he became leader of the Labour Party, had been blessed with good fortune. He had won everything for which he had striven – from the election as President of the Cardiff Students' Union in 1965 to the Labour leadership contest itself. The difficulties of leading his party out of opposition and into government must present him with unfamiliar challenges and pressures. But the drive which pushed him to the top so quickly has not deserted him. He told me he wanted to be off the island within forty-eight hours of arriving there. Obviously it takes more than eight records and a few domestic reflections to prevent Mr Kinnock from wading back into the thick of it.

"Laughing and loving are the two greatest things that
human beings can do."

Success may have eluded him at a general election, but Neil Kinnock does not consider himself to be an unlucky man. Throughout our interview he reviewed his past life and looked forward to the future with great optimism and verve. I'm sure there are many people who would dismiss all this as the predictable act of a skilful politician. I don't agree. I don't know whether Neil Kinnock will ever become Prime Minister, but I feel certain that his loyalty to his family and his background is deep and genuine. A man with such an anchor is bound to be confident – and likely to be optimistic too.

"I was very fortunate in my upbringing," he said at the start of the programme. "I'm still a very fortunate person in my family." He didn't dismiss out of hand the idea of 'luck' as a factor in the fortunes of men, but he had a pragmatic view of it. "I think luck comes out of hard work as often as not. Then it's always useful. Napoleon said: 'Give me lucky generals.' I believe the same thing." From luck we turned to fate. Were his views here much the same? "I think to depend on fate is a mistake. Some things come to nothing, others actually work. It's a mixture of luck and planning right down the line."

Neil Kinnock was born the son of a miner and a district nurse in the Welsh constituency of one of Britain's socialist heroes, Aneurin Bevan. He didn't know the great man, although he met him once or twice. "He was always a great figure up there as far as I was concerned, both physically and ideologically."

Just as important were his parents. Marvellous people, "totally committed to me and to the family and to the community – and they were always outward looking". They weren't politically active – at any rate, not until his mother retired.

"She was a district nurse and worked for the Monmouthshire County Council and had decided very early on that, despite being a very strong socialist, she'd never join the Labour Party whilst working. She didn't want anybody thinking that she'd gain preferment as a consequence of political contact. The idea that anyone would think my mother got preferment as a district nurse was daft. But the moment that she finished work, she and my father went down to the ward and joined the Labour Party. It was typical of them to do it in that way."

His father worked hard, doing tough jobs and putting in long hours. He was a good trade unionist, not terribly active, and "as long as they were paying him he was prepared to go to work". Life was comfortable if not luxurious. "Most years we had a holiday. We lived in a prefab and I was never conscious of any real shortage of money. We never had a car –

and I was fifteen when I bought our first television set, for ten quid, second-hand. But it couldn't have been thought of in any way as a poor household."

Young Neil was not a model schoolboy.

"It would irritate me immensely if my own children took the same attitude towards school. I think one of the problems was that I did very well at the eleven-plus. And like a lot of other people with that kind of success from that generation, decided, subconsciously, that that was it. Here we were, in this super-duper grammar school with a smart uniform, teachers in gowns and a terrific emphasis on academic success. It was all going to be all right. And when I woke up three years later it wasn't all right."

It may not have been all right, but it didn't sound all wrong either. Mr Kinnock struck me as someone who knows how to make the best of things. "I had a lot of fun," he admitted. He didn't have any idea of what he wanted to do. Disliking school intensely, he toyed with the idea of becoming a soldier, a policeman and a coal miner. "I took all the initial steps in every single case. When my parents discovered, there was hell." So was it their dedication which had prevented him from ending up being a decent beer-and-rugby valleys' lad? Mr Kinnock says not. He acknowledges his parents' influence – but feels sure there was something else too. "It sounds pious to say so – but since I think it, I might as well say it: there were always other things to be done, targets to be achieved. The main thrust was a political commitment." He joined the Labour Party when he was not yet fifteen years of age.

The idea of becoming an MP, however, was very distant and although he came to know some of Labour's leading figures, such as James Callaghan, Cledwyn Hughes and Michael Foot, the thought that he would one day follow them to the House of Commons was not really in his mind. "I thought my activity would be at a different level."

We paused here to talk more about his parents. He'd chosen as one of his records Heddle Nash singing the Serenade from Bizet's *Fair Maid of Perth*. It was his mother's favourite – "a beautiful song, so reminiscent of so much about home that it would be the kind of thing I'd want to take with me if I was going to be stuck by myself for a long time". This closeness to his parents was broken in 1971 when both of them died within a few days of each other. He doesn't think it was coincidence.

"I think my mother literally died of a broken heart. She had suffered from asthma very severely right from the winter of 1947. She never looked after herself properly, always kept working, and that gave her various kinds of weaknesses. My father had suffered from hypertension and some heart trouble right from his late fifties – that's not unusual. He eventually died after a week in hospital and then I think the strain and awful sense of grief

167

was too much for my mother and she died in seconds. And whilst I was with my father when he died, I didn't get to my mother until just after she died. It was a searing experience, and obviously the memory always lives with you. But I think the main memory, for myself and everybody else who knew them, is of them alive, very much alive."

Their deaths had come just a year after Neil Kinnock first became an MP. At least they'd seen him achieve that. They must, I thought, have been very proud. "They were, but typically they took it on the chin." He then told me how his mother had reacted when he rang to tell her that he'd been selected for the very safe seat of what was then called Bedwellty. His wife Glenys was six months' pregnant. "I've won," cried the excited victor down the telephone.

"Oh well, that's excellent. That's very good," came the motherly response. "Now you go home and make a nice cup of tea and get Glenys to put her feet up." His father, too, held young Neil's enthusiasm in check. "Westminster next stop, Dad," announced Mr Kinnock. "Oh you don't know", came the cautious reply. "People can be funny."

Neil Kinnock doesn't think his parents would ever have guessed that he'd become leader of the Labour Party. "My mother did have a speculation when I was a child, which the family used to rag her about, that I would be Viceroy of India." That job is no longer available, but Neil Kinnock has made up for it by choosing one that is equally – if not more – difficult.

It's a task which must be lightened by the presence of his wife Glenys, increasingly these days a public figure in her own right. I reminded him that what she remembers of their first meeting at Cardiff University was "a loud, ginger person" who offered her a leaflet and asked her for a date.

"Flattering as always, Glenys," admitted Mr Kinnock. "That was just how it happened – in the lunch queue. She took my eye immediately – and has been taking it ever since." Their partnership was described by a fellow student as "the power and the glory" in which Neil figured as the power and Glenys as the glory. "Subsequently, more mischievous profilers have turned it round so that she's become the power and I've become the glory. But she insists that the original sticks."

Nevertheless, there's no doubt that Glenys is a woman of considerable achievement. There are some who seem to think she's cleverer – or at any rate more canny – than her husband. Delicately, I asked whether he thought this could be true?

"I don't know, I've no idea. She's got all of the qualities that make women superior in so many departments, of that there is no doubt. And I think probably a little fey gift as well. Possibly something to do with coming from the Druids' country, Anglesey, I don't know what it is – a bit of second sight, I guess. Sometimes she will admit that I get things more right than she does more quickly, but getting an admission like that out of Glenys is quite an achievement. As for canniness, I think it really boils down to attitude towards people. There is a tendency for her to think the worst, and then be delighted when people demonstrate that they are of the best. My attitude is to look for the best and then be pretty vengeful when I discover the worst."

It was Glenys who led Neil to oratory. I had thought he possessed a natural passion for speaking, but he denied this. "I have no passion for speaking. I look forward to the day when I haven't got to make another single public speech." It was when he got to university that he took up public speaking seriously. Glenys told him that she quite liked people who debated and so – "to clinch the deal" – as he put it, he made a speech which apparently went down rather well. From then on, he just kept doing it. But his frequent speeches have brought with them the accusation of being a bit of a windbag. Did that upset him?

"Yes, because generally speaking it comes from people who have never been confronted with a requirement to make a real public speech in their life. Not some rehearsed and formal speech, or some witty after-dinner knockabout, but to really take issues head-on and have nothing but words and commitment to try and convince. It makes me a bit fed up, it'd be silly to say that it doesn't. But it can't be allowed to deflect or to diminish or to depress. That'd be foolish."

The fact that Neil Kinnock admitted to being hurt by such criticisms struck me as unusual in a politician. Certainly it contrasted oddly with the other charge that is sometimes made against him – that of ruthlessness. What were his feelings about that? He was ruthless, he replied, "only to the extent that there are objectives that need to be achieved in order to make our country more just and more productive. There are inhibitions that are largely self-inflicted by some people in the Labour movement. We've been through years of attempted persuasion, of encouragement, of conversation – and it still comes back to the exercise of vanity. People putting short-term interests before the objectives of securing change. So when they go and get in the way of that *objective*, not of me, I am fairly direct." And with directness (if not ruthlessness), great patience. Neil Kinnock's natural urges, I had thought, were to rush in and box someone who attacked him, but clearly the huge job of consolidating his party required more careful handling. Patience, he accepted, was necessary – and therefore he'd learned to acquire it.

"You see, the problem with this job is, I've had to exercise a degree of patience that I've never ever had to exercise in my life before. It's had to be exercised in order to ensure that when a purpose is set, it is actually achieved. Now it doesn't consist of death or glory rides – much as the press and other elements would quite like that. Life to them is a series of gunfights at the OK Corral, and life isn't really like that. So consequently, patiently and prudently, you set the objective and then you try and work things to get agreement, to see that people will accept it. And then implement it."

And the objective? What was that? The answer was forceful: "It's got to be a real bone-marrow feeling of unity. That's the kind of unity – not some cosmetic idea – that I want."

Neil Kinnock has shown enormous purposefulness in attempting to heal the divisions in his party and bring it before the electorate as a strengthened, trustworthy force. He once said that he'd only be happy in that task when he saw the furniture van move into Downing Street. As we came towards the end of the programme I asked him whether he thought that was ever likely to happen. "Oh it's going to happen very definitely," came the breezy, confident answer. "It will happen – because of basic values, and sense, and needs." But what if the change didn't happen in *his* time as leader of the party? His reply was once again assured. He dismissed the question: "I don't think that possibility arises, and in the meantime the development of democratic socialism in the Labour Party – in order to ensure that it's a compelling attraction providing a dependable political direction for the British people to take – is a real challenge. It's a challenge which is being fulfilled and I'm pleased to see that."

His last record took us back to his family. He had brought with him a tape recording he'd made of his daughter, Rachel, singing 'Horace the Horse' when she was two-and-a-half years old. It made him laugh: "laughing and loving are the two greatest things that human beings can do". It was the record he wanted as his favourite – a more down-to-earth form of relaxation than his book, which was R. H. Tawney's *Essays on Equality*. His luxury, chosen after that long, difficult deliberation, was Radio 4.

From everything Neil Kinnock had told me, I had to conclude that his political convictions were a natural part of him. Like his arch-rival, Margaret Thatcher, he looks into his own past to find the standards by which he judges the present. If you're a politician, where you come from can be just as important as what you think.

Neil Kinnock

Bryn Calfaria (Welsh hymn)
'Di quella pira' from *Il Trovatore* (Verdi)
Serenade from *The Fair Maid of Perth* (Bizet) – Heddle Nash
Symphony No. 1 (Brahms)
Wake Up Little Susie – Simon and Garfunkel
Imagine – John Lennon
Yada Yada – Dory Previn
**Horace the Horse – sung by Rachel Kinnock
(the castaway's daughter, aged 2½)**

Book: *Essays on Equality* (R. H. Tawney)

Luxury: *Radio 4*

DAME EDNA EVERAGE

Words alone cannot express the feelings of delight and anticipation which I felt when I learned that Dame Edna Everage had agreed to appear on *Desert Island Discs*. I was surprised that someone so busy could spare the time – and a little worried that she would not feel able to unburden herself as some of my other guests had done.

In the event, my fears were groundless. Dame Edna sailed through it, as she has through everything else. With a modest smile here, a secret thought there and a wicked little aside everywhere else, she rode in triumph through the bowels of Broadcasting House. She is a marvellous mixture of the homespun and the glamorous, the ordinary and the great. Those are the combinations which make her presence unique and her wisdom invaluable. She guides, she inspires – and yet she makes us laugh. What is her secret? Will we ever know?

"I am the acceptable face of feminism."

Dame Edna was gracious from the outset. Her first words were to thank me for the kind things I had said about her in my introduction to the programme. They had, she said, "touched me very, very deeply". I was thrilled.

She then proceeded to explain how she would react to life on the desert island. It would "remind me of the inner loneliness of the mega-star". I thought that was a very moving sentiment, displaying an understanding which one doesn't always find among the truly great. But then, as she reminded me, Dame Edna is a coper. "I think I've got a few little enzymes in me, not to say hormones, which would enable me to carve out a pretty rough existence for myself on a desert island. And remember – I was *born* on a desert island. Australia!" Of course she was. Somehow I'd never thought of it that way before.

Dame Edna chose music sung by women, including other famous daughters of her homeland such as Dame Nellie Melba, Dame Joan Sutherland and, from nearby New Zealand, Dame Kiri Te Kanawa. It was a decision, she explained, based on the fact that she was a bit of a feminist. "I'm the acceptable face of feminism," she told me with pride – and I thought how true that was. It was a position earned by her tireless work in the cause, a cause which demanded her to parade in public all the time. Had she always been able to do this? The answer was revealing.

"I was a shy child. I still am a shy woman. People think of me as so upfront, even brash, but in reality I'm deeply vulnerable and shy." She remembers that as a child she was too shy to sing to her aunties the songs she'd learned at school. "I had to hide behind the curtains in our lounge and pretend to be the wireless. I'd blush and I'd be tongue-tied and they'd pop me behind the curtains and say: 'Pretend to be the wireless, Edna' – and my bell-like notes would come out through them."

Of course, I wanted to know how a child so shy became such a star. It was the obvious question and tentatively (for in the presence of Dame Edna one often feels quite tentative) I asked it. The answer came effortlessly: "I was born a star." And she went on to explain that when her mother was in the maternity ward and asked, as soon as Edna had been delivered, "What is it?", the nurse had answered, "I think it's a mega-star."

Although shy, the young child learned to overcome her retiring nature and gradually gained confidence. Eventually spotted in a passion play in the rôle of Mary Magdalene – "I was cast against type there" – she was snapped up by a talent scout who set her on the road to her present success. This wonderful story shows, I think, how those who know their true selves can overcome obstacles strewn in their way and eventually attain great heights. Dame Edna is more than a mega-star: she is a guiding light.

Next we tackled a sensitive issue. On her shows, Dame Edna, for all her mercies, can be a hard taskmaster. At first she denied this, but I reminded her that she once damaged Larry Hagman by dropping him through the floor on her television programme.

"That's called 'tough love'," she said. "Was your mother all the time adoring and stroking you, or did she sometimes give you a little smack on your bottie?"

I had to admit that sometimes she did.

"And the rough edge of her tongue from time to time?"

Again, it was true. (Oh how painful it is to sit in front of the truly perceptive!)

"Not because she was being horrible to you," went on Dame Edna, "but because it was her way of caring, her way of loving you. A little 'tongue love' never did a kiddie any harm. And it never hurt an audience. And if these people think they can come in off the street and misbehave in my shows, eat chockies, take flashlight photographs and let their attention wander for a second – I'm sorry, I will not tolerate it."

With that stern warning we moved on. I asked her when she got her damehood, but she couldn't remember exactly. She told me it was for services to world culture and for helping cement the ties between England and Australia: "Let's face it, I'm Australian royalty." It had been "a marvellous moment" for her which had helped her career. But there were disadvantages too: "I think when you're a dame you have to tip people a bit more – so if it's ever Dame Sue Lawley remember, darling, you have to dip just a little bit deeper." Was that a rather common way to react to the dignity of such honour, I thought? But no: Dame Edna is many things, but never common. This was just another of her typically refreshing Antipodean *aperçus*.

Dame Edna has had to cope with many family problems. She grew a little irritable when I began to ask her about some of these. "Why are you digging away?" she blurted out suddenly – but then in a flood of that honest emotion which is so much her trademark, talked a little about the difficulties she's faced with her daughter, Valmay, a disturbed and troubled girl. Her kleptomania has resulted in shoplifting charges from time to time. In overcoming this domestic tragedy Dame Edna had, she said, been helped enormously by her public.

"I blamed myself. I'm one of those people that, if there's a bit of guilt lying around, I'll pick it up. You know those people who get up in the morning, clean their teeth and put on their shoes and when they go out of the door they say, 'Wait a minute, I've forgotten something'. Then they run back, pick up a big haversack of guilt and put it on their back and carry it through the day. You don't need to do that – misery is optional, possums."

Dame Edna is happy to acknowledge that she's beautiful. She's proud of it. "I'm a very physical woman, and I'm lucky because although I've got a few little spots where I think Dame Nature could have perhaps performed a few miracles, and didn't, I'm proud of my figure. I'm not ashamed of being beautiful." She describes herself as "statuesque" – an appropriate, Edna-like word for someone who stands six foot two inches in her heels. She has all her clothes made for her these days – the wealth which fame has brought her allows her to indulge in having what she wants to wear – and although she's under constant stress and lives off her nerves, she keeps herself in perfect condition. "People want to touch me, they say, 'What a beautiful skin you've got'. And I have." Then, in one of the most intimate and warm moments that I can ever remember on this or any other programme, she asked me to touch her. "Feel it. Feel this," she urged – referring to her skin, of course. And so it was that in a disagreeable basement studio, surrounded by the grime of ordinary men and women, I touched the velvet surface of one of the great people of our time.

"It's lovely," I said.

After such a moment as this there was little more to be said. Dame Edna admitted that her heart was still in the Melbourne suburb where she spent the first years of married life and where her husband, Norm, "had his earliest urological twinges". She confessed, too, that her great talent was not *hers* but something lent to her which, if she did not share with others, would "be repossessed like the vacuum cleaner by the finance company". And finally, in a beautiful moment of unsurpassed humility, she admitted that her instincts were still those of a suburban housewife. "I am still metaphorically up to my wrists in washing-up water," she told me. "I still wear spiritual Marigolds."

And so our conversation drew to a close. Her book was her "chubby old filofax – crammed with all the gorgeous things that I do and the names of my friends". Her luxury was her friend and lifelong companion, Madge Allsop. At first I demurred, explaining that human beings weren't allowed, that the luxury had to be an inanimate object. Dame Edna lowered her voice: "I can assure you, Madge is an inanimate object."

"You promise?" I asked, still uncertain.

"Well, when I saw her last she was pretty well comatose."

"In that case," I cried, "I shall make an exception!"

So it was that Dame Edna was given her wish. In lonely exile, as in her crowded life, that which she most desired could not be denied her.

Dame Edna Everage

Home Sweet Home – Dame Nellie Melba
If I Had a Talking Picture of You – Dame Joan Sutherland
**I Feel Pretty (*West Side Story*) –
Dame Kiri Te Kanawa**
Sex Appeal – Margo Lion
Wish Me Luck As You Wave Me Goodbye – Gracie Fields
It's Raining Sunbeams – Deanna Durbin
A Little King Without a Crown – Dame Vera Lynn
My Bridesmaid and I – Dame Edna Everage

Book: *Her filofax*

Luxury: *Madge Allsop*

APPENDIX

The date of the programme's first transmission on BBC Radio 4 is given in brackets after the castaway's name.

My castaways' records are printed in the order in which they were played on the programme. The piece of music they would choose in preference to the other seven is marked in bold type. Some recordings have special significance because of the occasion and the artists concerned: where possible, I have tried to indicate this by including additional information.

LORD HAILSHAM (March 27, 1988)

I Do Like to Be Beside the Seaside – Mark Sheridan
Swing Low Sweet Chariot – Paul Robeson
Dancing on the Ceiling – Jessie Matthews
'O frag mich nicht' from *The Faithful Peasant* (Fall) – Fritz Wunderlich
Regimental March of the Rifle Brigade
St Patrick's Breastplate (I Bind unto Myself Today)
'Vivat Regina' section from *I Was Glad* (Parry) – from the Coronation Service of Queen Elizabeth II
Dies irae (Gregorian chant)

Book: Works of Homer
Luxury: A bathtub and soap

JANE ASHER (April 3, 1988)

Penguin Parade (Herman Finck) – London Promenade Orchestra
The Arrival of the Queen of Sheba (Handel)
'Brightly Dawns our Wedding Day' from *The Mikado* (Gilbert and Sullivan)
Woman – Peter and Gordon
Without You – Harry Nilsson
'Dalla sua pace' from *Don Giovanni* (Mozart)
Kindergarten – Bill Cosby
'Ode to Joy' from Symphony No. 9, 'Choral' (Beethoven)

Book: *Tess of the d'Urbervilles* (Thomas Hardy)
Luxury: A hot bath with extra tap for cold champagne

ARTHUR SCARGILL (April 10, 1988)

The Entertainer (Scott Joplin)
Oh Love That Will Not Let Me Go (hymn)
Overture to *Orpheus in the Underworld* (Offenbach)
Beale Street Blues – Louis Armstrong and His All Stars
Old Shep – Elvis Presley
1812 Overture (Tchaikovsky) – Massed Brass Bands of Yorkshire
No Regrets – Edith Piaf
Chorus of the Hebrew Slaves from *Nabucco* (Verdi)

Book: *Huckleberry Finn* (Mark Twain)
Luxury: *The Mona Lisa*

MARY ARCHER (April 17, 1988)

Solemn Melody (Walford Davies) – George Thalben-Ball
'Onaway! Awake, Beloved' from *Hiawatha's Wedding Feast* (Coleridge-Taylor) – Richard
    Lewis
I Want to Hold Your Hand – The Beatles
Symphony No. 9, 'Choral' (Beethoven)
I Come from Heaven (carol)
This is the Record of John (Gibbons)
'Sanctus' from *Requiem* (Fauré)
Draw On, Sweet Night (Wilbye)

Book: *Remembrance of Things Past* (Marcel Proust)
Luxury: Needles, cotton and material

MICHAEL GAMBON (April 24, 1988)

Tutti Frutti – Little Richard
Othello's last speech (Shakespeare) – Sir Laurence Olivier
Breaking Down the Walls of Heartache – Johnny Johnson and the Bandwagon
Mistress Mine, Well May You Fare (Morley) – Peter Pears and Julian Bream
Woman – John Lennon
Memories of the Alhambra (Tárrega) – Narciso Yepes
Every Day a Little Death (*A Little Night Music*) – Maria Aitken
Symphony No. 7 (Beethoven)

Book: *Republican Party Reptile* (P. J. O'Rourke)
Luxury: Car (to listen to music in)

NEIL KINNOCK (May 1, 1988)

Bryn Calfaria (Welsh hymn)
'Di quella pira' from *Il Trovatore* (Verdi)
Serenade from *The Fair Maid of Perth* (Bizet) – Heddle Nash
Symphony No. 1 (Brahms)
Wake Up Little Susie – Simon and Garfunkel
Imagine – John Lennon
Yada Yada – Dory Previn
Horace the Horse – sung by Rachel Kinnock
   (the castaway's daughter, aged 2½)

Book: *Essays on Equality* (R. H. Tawney)
Luxury: Radio 4

PEGGY MAKINS (Evelyn Home) (May 8, 1988)

As Young As You Feel – Eileen Fowler
London Calls – Elsa Lanchester
A peal of 12 bells at Canterbury Cathedral
Ain't She Sweet – Jack Payne
Brandenburg Concerto No. 3 (Bach)
Se tu m'ami (Pergolesi) – Renata Tebaldi
The Shepherd on the Rock (Schubert)
Sinner, Please Don't Let This Harvest Pass – Paul Robeson

Book: The biggest atlas in the world
Luxury: A little rosebush

ROWAN ATKINSON (May 15, 1988)

Stairway to Heaven – Led Zeppelin
Miserere (Allegri) – Choir of King's College, Cambridge
Let It Be – The Beatles
Still Crazy After All These Years – Paul Simon
Miss Otis Regrets – Ella Fitzgerald
Nocturne in C sharp minor Op. 27 No. 1 (Chopin)
Every Time We Say Goodbye – Simply Red
Lady Writer – Dire Straits

Book: *Uncle Fred in Springtime* (P. G. Wodehouse)
Luxury: Car (to clean)

ANITA RODDICK (May 22, 1988)

Bachianas Brasileiras No. 5 (Villa-Lobos)
La bamba – Los Lobos
Concierto de Aranjuez (Rodrigo)
If I Could – Pat Metheny Group
Dancing in the Dark – Bruce Springsteen
Holding Back the Years – Simply Red
I Still Haven't Found What I'm Looking For – U2
Seduced – Mary Coughlan

Book: *Prince of Tides* (Pat Conroy)
Luxury: A comfortable bed with pillows and sheets

RABBI LIONEL BLUE (May 29, 1988)

My Yiddishe Momme – Sophie Tucker
Why Has a Cow Got Four Legs? – Cicely Courtneidge
Ich hab' noch einen Koffer in Berlin – Marlene Dietrich
Trio from *Der Rosenkavalier* (R. Strauss) – Elisabeth Schwarzkopf
Up Above My Head I Hear Music in the Air – Sister Rosetta Tharpe
Nobody Knows You When You're Down and Out – Bessie Smith
Requiem (Victoria) – Prague Madrigal Singers
Quartet for the End of Time (Messiaen)

Book: The biggest volume of pure maths
Luxury: A toilet bag with toothpaste, electric razor, etc.

ANTON MOSIMANN (June 5, 1988)

Overture to *William Tell* (Rossini)
Down by the Riverside – Golden Gate Quartet
Piano Quintet in A, 'Trout' (Schubert)
Diamonds Are Forever – Shirley Bassey
Memory *(Cats)* – Barbara Dickson
Overture to *The Barber of Seville* (Rossini)
Back o' Town Blues – Louis Armstrong and His All Stars
Super Trouper – Abba

Book: *Opera di M. Bartolomeo Scappi* (recipe book of Pope's chef in 1525)
Luxury: A steamer for cooking

DOUGLAS HURD (June 12, 1988)

Tales from the Vienna Woods (J. Strauss II)
For All the Saints (hymn, Vaughan Williams)
The White-haired Girl (Chinese opera)
'Tu che a Dio' from *Lucia di Lammermoor* (Donizetti)
The Hostess with the Mostes' – Ethel Merman
Easter Hymn from *Cavalleria Rusticana* (Mascagni)
Another Suitcase in Another Hall (*Evita*)
'In paradisum' from *Requiem* (Fauré)

Book: *The Oxford Book of Twentieth-Century Verse* (selected by Philip Larkin)
Luxury: Champagne

GWEN FFRANGCON-DAVIES (June 19, 1988)

Piano Quintet in A, 'Trout' (Schubert)
'Ich hab' ein glühend' Messer' from *Songs of a Wayfarer* (Mahler) – Dietrich Fischer-
   Dieskau
'Shepherds' Hymn after the Storm' from Symphony No. 6, 'Pastoral' (Beethoven)
'Fair Is the Moonlight' from *The Immortal Hour* (Rutland Boughton) – Gwen Ffrangcon-
   Davies
The Journey of the Magi (T. S. Eliot) – Sir John Gielgud
Double Violin Concerto (Bach)
Fanfare, from the Coronation of Queen Elizabeth II
'Liebestod' from *Tristan and Isolde* (Wagner) – Kirsten Flagstad

Book: No other book requested
Luxury: A large bottle of toilet water

JEREMY ISAACS (June 26, 1988)

Quartet from *Rigoletto* (Verdi)
Prologue from *Ariadne auf Naxos* (R. Strauss)
Trio from *Der Rosenkavalier* (R. Strauss)
Letter Duet from *The Marriage of Figaro* (Mozart)
Quartet from *Fidelio* (Beethoven)
String Quartet No. 19 in C 'Dissonance' (Mozart) – Amadeus Quartet
'Dunque io son' from *The Barber of Seville* (Rossini)
Final duet from *Jenůfa* (Janàcék)

Book: A compilation of Benny Green
Luxury: A frogman's outfit and snorkel

DR DAVID OWEN (July 3, 1988)

Enigma Variations (Elgar)
We'll Keep a Welcome in the Hillside
'When I Was a Lad' from *HMS Pinafore* (Gilbert and Sullivan)
Interesting Facts (sketch from *The Secret Policeman's Ball*) – Peter Cook and John Cleese
Little Brown Jug – Glenn Miller and His Orchestra
Lucy in the Sky with Diamonds – The Beatles
'Mack the Knife' from *The Threepenny Opera* (Weill) – Lotte Lenya
Piano Concerto No. 21 in C (Mozart)

Book: His own anthology of poems
Luxury: A hot bath

DAVID ESSEX (July 10, 1988)

'Jupiter' from *The Planets* (Holst)
Down Forget-Me-Not Lane – Flanagan and Allen
In My Life – The Beatles
God Only Knows – The Beach Boys
Pomp and Circumstance March No. 1 (Elgar)
Somewhere *(West Side Story)*
Time After Time – Cyndi Lauper
Tutti Frutti – Little Richard

Book: *The Guinness Book of Records*
Luxury: A set of cricket equipment

DAME EDNA EVERAGE (July 17, 1988)

Home Sweet Home – Dame Nellie Melba
If I Had a Talking Picture of You – Dame Joan Sutherland
I Feel Pretty (*West Side Story*) – Dame Kiri Te Kanawa
Sex Appeal – Margo Lion
Wish Me Luck As You Wave Me Goodbye – Gracie Fields
It's Raining Sunbeams – Deanna Durban
A Little King Without a Crown – Dame Vera Lynn
My Bridesmaid and I – Dame Edna Everage

Book: Her filofax
Luxury: Madge Allsop

LORD ARMSTRONG (July 24, 1988)

Mass in B minor (Bach)
Nell (Fauré) – Maggie Teyte
Mass for 5 Voices (Byrd) – Choir of Christ Church Cathedral, Oxford
Serenade to Music (Vaughan Williams)
The end of Act 2 of *The Mastersingers of Nuremberg* (Wagner)
Part of Act 1 of *Falstaff* (Verdi) – Mirella Freni and Alfredo Kraus
Piano Trio No. 1 in D minor (Mendelssohn)
Finale from Act 2 of *The Marriage of Figaro* (Mozart) – Mirella Freni and Wladimiro
    Ganzarolli

Book: Collected works of Jane Austen
Luxury: Music manuscript paper, pencil, rubber

JOAN TURNER (July 31, 1988)

The Shadow Waltz – Joan Turner
I've Got You under My Skin – Frank Sinatra
Edelweiss (*The Sound of Music*) – Vince Hill
'One Fine Day' from *Madam Butterfly* (Puccini)
I'll Walk with God – Mario Lanza
Tales of the Unexpected (theme music from the television series)
Bright Eyes – Art Garfunkel
'I Have Dreamed' from *The King and I* – Joan Turner

Book: *Introduction to the Devout Life* (St Francis de Sales)
Luxury: Baked beans

REV. IAN PAISLEY (August 7, 1988)

Psalm 23 – Reformed Presbyterian Church of Ireland Northern Presbytery Choir
Pull for the Shore – William MacEwan
Would You Be Free? – Congregation of Martyrs Memorial Church, Belfast
Danny Boy – Robert White
Bound for Texas Land – Killycoogan Accordion Band
Amazing Grace
Thy Way O Lord – Bertha Norman
When the Trumpet of the Lord Shall Sound – Rev. William McCrea

Book: Foxe's *Book of Martyrs*
Luxury: A high-powered radio

PATRICIA NEAL (August 14, 1988)

Rhapsody in Blue (Gershwin)
Toccata and Fugue in D minor (Bach)
Begin the Beguine – Ella Fitzgerald
La vie en rose – Edith Piaf
One for My Baby – Frank Sinatra
True Love (*High Society*) – Bing Crosby and Grace Kelly
Birmingham Jail – The Famous Nashville Artists
Black Is the Colour – Joan Baez

Book: A collection of short stories
Luxury: Toothbrush and toothpaste

LORD DACRE (August 21, 1988)

Piano Concerto No. 27 in B flat, K595 (Mozart)
Ombra mai fu (Largo) from *Xerxes* (Handel) – Kathleen Ferrier
'Traurigkeit' from *The Abduction from the Seraglio* (Mozart) – Edita Gruberová
Sheep May Safely Graze (Bach) – Emma Kirkby
Siegfried Idyll (Wagner)
Pavane for a Dead Infanta (Ravel)
Divertimento for Strings (Bartók)
The opening of Symphony No. 6, 'Pastoral' (Beethoven)

Book: Collected works of Virgil
Luxury: Paper, pen and ink

ANITA DOBSON (August 28, 1988)

The Locomotion – Little Eva
Cathy's Clown – The Everly Brothers
Please Please Me – The Beatles
Band of Gold – Freda Payne
Be My Baby – The Ronnettes
Bohemian Rhapsody – Queen
Thriller – Michael Jackson
What Do You Want? – Adam Faith

Book: *The Picture of Dorian Gray* (Oscar Wilde)
Luxury: A bed

A. WAINWRIGHT (September 4, 1988)

Tales from the Vienna Woods (J. Strauss II) – Richard Tauber
Smoke Gets in Your Eyes – Tommy Dorsey and His Orchestra
There's an Empty Cot in the Bunkhouse Tonight – Rex Allen
Come Back to Sorrento – Luciano Pavarotti
Oh, What a Beautiful Mornin' (*Oklahoma!*) – Gordon MacRae
The Happy Wanderer – Berkshire Boys Choir
Skye Boat Song – Kenneth McKellar
Somewhere My Love ('Lara's Theme' from *Dr Zhivago*) – Johnny Mathis

Book: No book, but two photographs – one of the 1928 Blackburn Rovers football team, the other of his wife, Betty
Luxury: A mirror (to watch his beard growing)

PETER DONOHOE (September 11, 1988)

Piano Concerto No. 5, 'Emperor' (Beethoven)
Side Saddle – Russ Conway
'Prize Song' from *The Mastersingers of Nuremberg* (Wagner) – René Kollo
Rhapsody in Blue (Gershwin) – Peter Donohoe
Piano Concerto No. 3 in D minor (Rachmaninov) – Peter Donohoe
Turangalîla Symphonie (Messiaen) – Peter Donohoe
Symphony No. 3 (Brahms)
String Quintet in C (Schubert)

Book: Collected scripts of Billy Connolly
Luxury: A waterbed

SALMAN RUSHDIE (September 18, 1988)

Mera joota hai japani – Mukesh
Heartbreak Hotel – Elvis Presley
I-Feel-Like-I'm-Fixin'-to-Die Rag – Country Joe and the Fish
Improvisation on the theme music from *Pather Panchali* – Ravi Shankar
'Habañera' from *Carmen* (Bizet) – Maria Callas
Sympathy for the Devil – The Rolling Stones
Tum aaye ho na – Noor Jehan
Call of the Valley – Shivkumar Sharma

Book: *Arabian Nights*
Luxury: An unlisted radio telephone

MOST REV. TREVOR HUDDLESTON (September 25, 1988)

Symphony No. 9, 'New World' (Dvořák)
The Song of the Earth (Mahler)
Prisoners' Chorus from *Fidelio* (Beethoven)
Free Nelson Mandela – The Special AKA
'Sanctus' from *Requiem* (Fauré)
'Summertime' from *Porgy and Bess* (Gershwin)
'Gute Nacht' from *Die Winterreise* (Schubert)
Love Duet from *Otello* (Verdi)

Book: *The Oxford Book of English Verse*
Luxury: A pair of binoculars

ATHENE SEYLER (October 2, 1988)

Oh! Mr Porter – Norah Blaney
Du bist wie eine Blume (Schumann) – Dame Kiri Te Kanawa
Pack Up Your Troubles – Charles Chilton
Sally – Gracie Fields
Morning Has Broken – St Philip's Choir
Pop Goes the Weasel
Ol' Man River (*Showboat*) – Paul Robeson
Waltz in C sharp minor Op. 64 No. 2 (Chopin)

Book: *The Disinherited* (Gareth Jones)
Luxury: A case of champagne

TERRY WOGAN (October 9, 1988)

My Love Is Like a Red Red Rose – Irene Sharp
'Avant de quitter ces lieux' from *Faust* (Gounod)
Grand March from *Aida* (Verdi)
Nuns' Chorus from *Casanova* (J. Strauss II, arr. Benatzky)
When the Lighthouse Shines Across the Bay – Conrad Veidt
The Floral Dance – Brighouse and Rastrick Brass Band
'For the Merriest Fellows Are We' from *The Gondoliers* (Gilbert and Sullivan)
Stardust – Nat 'King' Cole

Book: *The Collected Works of P. G. Wodehouse*
Luxury: A radio/cassette player and language tapes

CILLA BLACK (October 16, 1988)

Introducing tobacco to civilisation – Bob Newhart
Everything I Own – Bread
Why Do Fools Fall in Love? – Frankie Lymon
Stay With Me – Lorraine Ellison
You Send Me – Sam Cooke
Long Tall Sally – Little Richard
Pomp and Circumstance March No. 1 (Elgar)
The Long and Winding Road – The Beatles

Book: *Aesop's Fables*
Luxury: A manicure set and nail varnish

MICHAEL FOOT (October 23, 1988)

Piano Concerto No. 23 in A, K488 (Mozart) – Solomon
'Una voce poco fa' from The Barber of Seville (Rossini)
'Se vuol ballare' from *The Marriage of Figaro* (Mozart)
Hunting Dance from *Love in Bath* (Handel, arr. Beecham)
Symphony No. 6, 'Pastoral' (Beethoven)
Myfanwy – Massed Male Voice Choirs of Monmouthshire
Lindoro's Song from *The Italian Girl in Algiers* (Rossini)

Book: *Don Juan* (Lord Byron)
Luxury: An alarm clock encased in Welsh tinplate

GERMAINE GREER (October 30, 1988)

Popule meus, quid feci tibi? (Victoria)
Prologue to *The Play of Daniel* (12th century, anon.)
Pueri concinite – Placido Domingo and the Vienna Boys Choir
Habayta – Shoshana Damari
Pièces de Clavecin (Couperin)
'Beim Schlafengehen' from *Four Last Songs* (R. Strauss)
Vuelve a sacudirse el continente – Pablo Milanes and Silvio Rodriguez
An Ethiopian pop song – Neway Debebe

Book: *The Oxford English Dictionary*
Luxury: Hot spices

SIR CLAUS MOSER (November 6, 1988)

Trio in B flat Op. 97, 'Archduke' (Beethoven)
Bénédiction de Dieu dans la solitude (Liszt) – Louis Kentner
String Quintet in G minor (Mozart)
Fantasia in F minor Op. 103 (Schubert)
Double Violin Concerto (Bach)
Vespers (Monteverdi)
Wotan's Farewell from *Die Walküre* (Wagner)
Sextet from *The Marriage of Figaro* (Mozart)

Book: A volume of James Thurber
Luxury: A Steinway grand piano

BOB HOSKINS (November 13, 1988)

When I See an Elephant Fly – Crow Quintet and orchestra
Bad Penny Blues – Humphrey Lyttelton and His Band
What'd I Say – Ray Charles
Honky Tonk Woman – The Rolling Stones
Priests' Chorus from *The Magic Flute* (Mozart)
Imagine – John Lennon
Moanin' – Lambert, Hendricks and Ross
Adagio for Strings (Barber)

Book: *Catch 22* (Joseph Heller)
Luxury: A telescope

BOB CHAMPION (November 20, 1988)

With or Without You – U2
If I Were a Carpenter – The Four Tops
Bridge over Troubled Water – Simon and Garfunkel
Champions (theme music from the film)
Happy Christmas – John Lennon and Yoko Ono
Sailing – Rod Stewart
Satisfaction – The Rolling Stones
Galveston – Glen Campbell

Book: *Fraser's Horse Book* by Frank Manolson and Alistair Fraser
Luxury: A bronze statue of the racehorse 'Aldaniti'

STEPHEN FRY (November 27, 1988)

Champagne Aria from *Don Giovanni* (Mozart)
Shirt – Bonzo Dog Band
'Non più andrai' from *The Marriage of Figaro* (Mozart)
I've Got You under My Skin – Frank Sinatra and the Count Basie Orchestra
Bat Out of Hell – Meatloaf
Magic Fire Music from *Die Walküre* (Wagner)
Quartet from *Rigoletto* (Verdi)
'Liebestod' from *Tristan and Isolde* (Wagner)

Book: *The Jeeves Omnibus* (P. G. Wodehouse)
Luxury: A suicide pill

LADY WARNOCK (December 4, 1988)

Serenade No. 12 in C minor (Mozart)
'Denn alles Fleisch es ist wie Gras' from *A German Requiem* (Brahms)
Bye Bye Love – The Everly Brothers
Concerto Grosso No. 2 (Handel)
My Beloved Spake (Purcell)
Auf dem Strom (Schubert)
Cantata No. 4, 'Christ lag in Todesbanden' (Bach)
Trio Sonata No. 3 in B flat (Zelenka)

Book: *The Last Chronicle of Barset* (Anthony Trollope)
Luxury: Pen and paper

CHARLES DANCE (December 11, 1988)

Sweet Little Sixteen – Chuck Berry
Nobody Told Me – John Lennon
The Dark Island – The First Battalion Scots Guard
Piano Sonata No. 23 in F minor, 'Appassionata' (Beethoven)
Concerto for 2 Mandolins and Strings (Vivaldi)
Drive – The Cars
Good Morning Babylon (theme music from the film)
Silent Night – Bach Choir

Book: *A Dream in the Luxembourg* (Richard Aldington)
Luxury: A guitar

EDWARD HEATH (December 18, 1988)

A Sea Symphony (Vaughan Williams)
Piano Trio in B flat Op. 99 (Schubert)
Trio from *Der Rosenkavalier* (R. Strauss)
If I Were a Rich Man *(Fiddler on the Roof)* – Topol
'Cockaigne' Overture (Elgar) – London Symphony Orchestra conducted by Edward Heath
Prisoners' Chorus from *Fidelio* (Beethoven)
Symphony No. 9, 'New World' (Dvořák)
Hark the Herald Angels Sing

Book: A volume of the works of the Impressionist painters
Luxury: Suntan lotion

MOST REV. ROBERT RUNCIE (January 1, 1989)

'Sea Slumber Song' from *Sea Pictures* (Elgar) – Dame Janet Baker
Dinah – Fats Waller
Regimental March of the Scots Guard (Hielan' Laddie)
Love Duet from *La Bohème* (Puccini)
The Lark Ascending (Vaughan Williams)
'Laudate dominum' from *Vespers*, K339 (Mozart)
In the Bleak Mid-winter – Canterbury Cathedral Choir
'Sanctus' from Mass in B minor (Bach)

Book: *The Odyssey* (Homer)
Luxury: His own rocking chair

TWIGGY (January 8, 1989)

The Laughing Policeman – Charles Penrose
Yesterday – The Beatles
Adagio in G minor (Albinoni)
'Mira, O Norma' from *Norma* (Bellini)
Ten Cents a Dance – Ruth Etting
Adagio from *Concierto de Aranjuez* (Rodrigo)
On My Own *(Les Misérables)* – Frances Ruffelle
I Will Love You Every Time – The Fureys

Book: *Tess of the d'Urbervilles* (Thomas Hardy)
Luxury: Cold cream

TONY BENN (January 15, 1989)

He Who Would Valiant Be
'Lord God of Abraham' from *Elijah* (Mendelssohn) – Paul Robeson
Slow Train – Michael Flanders and Donald Swann
Sheep May Safely Graze (Bach) – Kirsten Flagstad
Joe Hill – Joan Baez
We Shall Overcome – Mahalia Jackson
A madrigal (composed by Stephen Benn)
The World Turned Upside Down – Leon Rosselson and Roy Bailey

Book: *Das Kapital* (Karl Marx)
Luxury: A kettle and teabags

BOY GEORGE (January 22, 1989)

Blowin' in the Wind – Marlene Dietrich
It Must Be Love – Madness
If I Were Your Woman – Gladys Knight and the Pips
Life's a Gas – Marc Bolan
Stormy Weather – Elisabeth Welch
When a Woman Loves a Man – Ella Fitzgerald
Woman to Woman – Shirley Brown
War Baby – Tom Robinson

Book: A photograph album
Luxury: A radio

JOAN ARMATRADING (January 29, 1989)

Violin Concerto in E minor (Mendelssohn)
That Old Black Magic – Ella Fitzgerald
Madame George – Van Morrison
Symphony No. 4 (Mahler)
The Magnificent Seven (theme music from the film)
'Dies irae' from *Requiem* (Verdi)
I'm a Man – Muddy Waters
Symphony No. 9, 'New World' (Dvořák)

Book: *Why Didn't They Ask Evans?* (Agatha Christie)
Luxury: A guitar

ROCCO FORTE (February 5, 1989)

O surdato 'nnammurato (Neapolitan song)
Good Golly Miss Molly – Little Richard
Jerusalem – Seaford College Chapel Choir
Unforgettable – Nat 'King' Cole
'Dies irae' from *Requiem* (Verdi)
Nocturne in B flat minor Op. 9 No. 1 (Chopin)
Symphony No. 5 (Beethoven)
'Habañera' from *Carmen* (Bizet) – Maria Callas

Book: *The Divine Comedy* (Dante)
Luxury: A snooker table

JEFFREY TATE (February 12, 1989)

Poor Little Rich Girl – Noël Coward
'Villes' from *Les Illuminations* (Britten) – Peter Pears
In the Bleak Mid-winter – Choir of King's College, Cambridge
The Banks of Green Willow (Butterworth) – English Chamber Orchestra conducted
    by Jeffrey Tate
Quintet from *Così fan tutte* (Mozart)
Symphony No. 104, 'London' (Haydn)
'Fliedermonolog' from *The Mastersingers of Nuremberg* (Wagner)
I'll Be Seeing You – Billie Holiday

Book: Collected works of Jane Austen
Luxury: *The Nativity* (painting by Piero della Francesca)

ENOCH POWELL (February 19, 1989)

'Entry of the Gods into Valhalla' from *Rheingold* (Wagner)
'Siegmund's Spring Song' from *Die Walküre* (Wagner)
'Siegfried's Forging Song' from *Siegfried* (Wagner)
'Renunciation of Siegfried' from *Twilight of the Gods* (Wagner)
Symphony No. 6, 'Pastoral' (Beethoven)
Symphony No. 9, 'Choral' (Beethoven)
Prisoners' Chorus from *Fidelio* (Beethoven)
'In Native Worth and Honour Clad' from *The Creation* (Haydn)

Book: The *Old Testament* (in Hebrew) and the *New Testament* (in Greek)
Luxury: A fish smoker

DAVID HARE (February 26, 1989)

Double Violin Concerto (Bach)
Young and Foolish – Mabel Mercer
String Quartet No. 16 in F (Beethoven)
Jole Blon – Gary U.S. Bonds
The Rite of Spring (Stravinsky)
'One Life to Live' from *Lady in the Dark* (Weill)
Transfigured Night (Schoenberg)
Younger than Springtime *(South Pacific)* – Mandy Patinkin

Book: *Larousse Gastronomique*
Luxury: A cricket bat and bowling machine

DAME JOSEPHINE BARNES (March 5, 1989)

Fantasia and Fugue in G minor (Bach)
Concerto in F for 3 pianos (Mozart)
'Der Lindenbaum' from *Die Winterreise* (Schubert)
String Quartet No. 16 in F (Beethoven)
Komm, Jesu, komm! (Bach)
Cello Concerto (Elgar)
Act 3 of *Falstaff* (Verdi)
I Was Glad (Parry) – from the Coronation Service of Queen Elizabeth II

Book: The scores of all her chosen music bound in one volume
Luxury: A solar-powered word processor

GERALD SCARFE (March 12, 1989)

Bless You for Being an Angel – The Ink Spots
La mer – Charles Trenet
Art Gallery (sketch) – Peter Cook and Dudley Moore
Nocturne in E flat Op. 9 No. 2 (Chopin)
Cello Suite No. 1 in G (Bach)
Prologue to *Under Milk Wood* (Dylan Thomas) – Richard Burton
The penultimate scene of *Don Giovanni* (Mozart)
Prelude to Act 1 of *Die Walküre* (Wagner)

Book: A book by Capability Brown
Luxury: A river painting by Turner

SIR STEPHEN SPENDER (April 2, 1989)

Act 2 of *Falstaff* (Verdi)
String Quartet No. 15 in A minor (Beethoven)
Act 1 of *The Rake's Progress* (Stravinsky)
I'm a Tree – Douglas Byng
Allegretto from Piano Sonata No. 20 in A, D959 (Schubert)
Piano Concerto No. 2 in B flat (Beethoven) – Natasha Litvin (the castaway's wife)
String Quartet in F minor Op. 20 No. 5 (Haydn)
Act 3 of *Twilight of the Gods* (Wagner)

Book: *Remembrance of Things Past* (Marcel Proust)
Luxury: A painting or sculpture by his son, Matthew, with a photograph of his daughter,
    Lizzie, stuck on the back

LESLIE GRANTHAM (April 9, 1989)

Limelight (theme music from the film)
Rose Marie – Slim Whitman
Danny Boy – Jackie Wilson
The Test Pilot (sketch from 'Hancock's Half Hour')
Heartbeat – Buddy Holly
Love Walked In – Kenny Baker and Andrea Leeds
Object of My Affection – Pinky Tomlin
Every Time We Say Goodbye – Simply Red

Book: *Robinson Crusoe* (Daniel Defoe)
Luxury: A metal detector

LORD JENKINS (April 16, 1989)

We'll Keep a Welcome in the Hillside
Soviet Airman's Song
Enigma Variations (Elgar)
'Printemps qui commence' from *Samson and Delilah* (Saint-Saëns)
Prelude to *A Masked Ball* (Verdi)
Chariots of Fire – Vangelis
'The Land of the Mountain and the Flood' Overture (Hamish MacCunn)
Symphony No. 92, 'Oxford' (Haydn)

Book: *Who Was Who*
Luxury: A case of Bordeaux wine

MIRIAM ROTHSCHILD (April 23, 1989)

If You Were the only Girl in the World – Anne Ziegler and Webster Booth
Some Enchanted Evening (*South Pacific*) – Paul Robeson
My Lindy Lou – Paul Robeson
Prelude from Cello Suite No. 5 in C minor (Bach)
Recording of a nightingale singing
Fantasia in D minor for 4 viols (Purcell) – Concentus Musicus, Vienna
Somewhere My Love ('Lara's Theme' from *Dr Zhivago*) – Roger Whittaker
The Lambeth Walk – Teddie St Denis and Lupino Lane

Book: *Encyclopaedia Britannica*
Luxury: A packet of wildflower seeds

RACHEL KEMPSON, LADY REDGRAVE (April 30, 1989)

Piano Quintet in A, 'Trout' (Schubert)
Andante from the *Water Music* (Handel)
If the Heart of a Man (*The Beggar's Opera*) – Michael Redgrave
'Spring' from *The Four Seasons* (Vivaldi)
What Do the Simple Folk Do? (*Camelot*) – Vanessa Redgrave and Richard Harris
Adam Lay ybounden (carol)
Adagietto from Symphony No. 5 (Mahler)
Prelude to *Werther* (Massenet)

Book: *Jane Eyre* (Charlotte Brontë)
Luxury: A case of champagne

LENNY HENRY (May 7, 1989)

Kiss – Prince
13-question Method – Ry Cooder
Is This Love – Bob Marley and the Wailers
Company – Rickie Lee Jones
I'd Rather Be With You – Bootsy Collins
I Just Called to Say I Love You – Stevie Wonder
Shipbuilding – Robert Wyatt
One Nation Under a Groove – Funkadelic

Book: *Catch 22* (Joseph Heller)
Luxury: 'Graphic novels' (comics)

THORA HIRD (May 14, 1989)

Temptation Rag – Pasadena Roof Orchestra
Blaze Away – Royal Artillery Band
Gold and Silver Waltz (Lehár) – Johann Strauss Orchestra of Vienna
Cumberland Gap – Lonnie Donegan
None but the Lonely Heart (Tchaikovsky)
When the Saints Go Marching In
Andante from Piano Concerto No. 21 in C (Mozart) – Richard Clayderman
Onward Christian Soldiers

Book: *Scene and Hird* (Thora Hird)
Luxury: Cleansing milk

KATHARINE HAMNETT (May 21, 1989)

Rise to the Occasion – Climie Fisher
Big Head – Max Bygraves
The Trail of the Lonesome Pine – Laurel and Hardy
You Can't Always Get What You Want – The Rolling Stones
Walk This Way – Run DMC
Madam Butterfly (One Fine Day) – Malcolm McLaren
Bonjour Titi, Salut Sylvestre – Titi and Sylvestre
Jerusalem

Book: The *I Ching*
Luxury: An aircraft carrier

SIR NICHOLAS HENDERSON (May 28, 1989)

'Winter' from *The Four Seasons* (Vivaldi)
Night and Day – Fred Astaire
Overture to *Die Fledermaus* (J. Strauss II)
Horn Concerto No. 3 (Mozart)
Barcarolle in F sharp minor (Chopin)
Piano Concerto No. 19 in F (Mozart)
Extract from *The Clicking of Cuthbert* (P. G. Wodehouse) – Timothy Carlton
Waltz in G (Brahms) – Benjamin Moore (the castaway's grandson, aged six)

Book: Guy de Maupassant's short stories
Luxury: A sculpture from the Louvre and a large packet of seeds

RICHARD BRANSON (June 4, 1989)

Summer Holiday – Cliff Richard
Goodness Gracious Me – Peter Sellers and Sophia Loren
You're a Lady – Peter Skellern
Fever – Peggy Lee
Tubular Bells – Mike Oldfield
In the Air Tonight – Phil Collins
Do You Really Want to Hurt Me? – Culture Club
She's a Mystery to Me – Roy Orbison

Book: A teach-yourself Japanese phrase book/dictionary
Luxury: Notebooks and pens

JONATHON PORRITT (June 11, 1989)

Symphony No. 9, 'New World' (Dvořák)
Chariots of Fire – Vangelis
Nunc dimittis (Gregorian chant) – Choir of the Carmelite Priory, London
Samba pa ti – Santana
Hills of the North Rejoice
Humpback whale music
Bridge Over Troubled Water – Simon and Garfunkel
Piano Concerto No. 6 in B flat (Mozart)

Book: *Bleak House* (Charles Dickens)
Luxury: A fountain pen

MARIA AITKEN (June 18, 1989)

Mad About the Boy – Diane Langton
Three Little Fishes – The Andrews Sisters
Heartbreak Hotel – Elvis Presley
'Always True to You in My Fashion' from *Kiss Me Kate* – Ann Miller and Tommy Rall
'Parigi, O cara' from *La Traviata* (Verdi)
Ballade No. 2 in F (Chopin)
'Summertime' from *Porgy and Bess* (Gershwin)
'Pie Jesu' from *Requiem* (Fauré)

Book: *Fun in a Chinese Laundry* (Josef von Sternberg)
Luxury: Amazonian rain-maker

JOAN COLLINS (June 25, 1989)

Come Back to Sorrento – Luciano Pavarotti
We'll Meet Again – Dame Vera Lynn
The Wonder of You – Elvis Presley
Come Fly With Me – Frank Sinatra
Intermezzo from *Manon Lescaut* (Puccini)
All I Ask of You (*The Phantom of the Opera*) – Steve Barton and Sarah Brightman
'O mio babbino caro' from *Gianni Schicchi* (Puccini)
Love Will Conquer All – Lionel Richie

Book: *The Picture of Dorian Gray* (Oscar Wilde)
Luxury: A large bottle of moisturiser

MARK MCCORMACK (July 2, 1989)

Don't Cry for Me, Argentina (*Evita*) – Julie Covington
And I Love Her – The Beatles
Best of My Love – The Eagles
Both Sides Now – Tony Jacklin
Drive All Night – Bruce Springsteen
Leather and Lace – Stevie Nicks
Mull of Kintyre – Wings
Candle in the Wind – Elton John

Book: *Les Misérables* (Victor Hugo), with a French dictionary
Luxury: Suntan lotion

NED SHERRIN (July 9, 1989)

Up from Somerset – Peter Dawson
As Time Goes By – Elisabeth Welch
Gymnopédie No. 1 (Satie)
You Don't Know What It's Like to Fall in Love at Forty (*Sing a Rude Song*, book and
    lyrics by Caryl Brahms and Ned Sherrin) – Barbara Windsor
Woman Talk (lyric by Caryl Brahms) – Cleo Laine
Side by Side by Side (Sondheim) – Millicent Martin
Why Do People Fall in Love? (*The Mitford Girls*, book and lyrics by Caryl Brahms and
    Ned Sherrin) – Patricia Hodge
Not Funny (lyric by Ned Sherrin) – Marion Montgomery

Book: *No Bed for Bacon* (Caryl Brahms)
Luxury: A sack of seed potatoes

SIR THOMAS ARMSTRONG (July 16, 1989)

'Comfort ye, my people' from *Messiah* (Handel)
L'Ile joyeuse (Debussy)
Ganymed (Schubert)
Brigg Fair (Delius)
Fantasia on a Theme of Thomas Tallis (Vaughan Williams)
The Rio Grande (Constant Lambert) – conducted by the composer
The Wilderness (S. S. Wesley)
'Sanctus' from Mass in B minor (Bach)

Book: No other book requested
Luxury: A clavichord

DAME VERA LYNN (September 3, 1989)

Room 504 – Dame Vera Lynn
A Man and His Dream – Artie Shaw and His Orchestra
Memory *(Cats)* – Elaine Paige
Till There Was You – The Beatles
Where the Blue of the Night – Bing Crosby
Adagio for Strings (Barber)
Chi mai (theme music from the television series *The Life and Times of David Lloyd George*)
Heart of Gold – Vera Lynn and Charlie Kunz

Book: A book of edible fruits and vegetables
Luxury: Watercolour paints, brushes and paper

ERIC CLAPTON (September 10, 1989)

'Senza mamma' from *Suor Angelica* (Puccini)
Duet from *The Pearl Fishers* (Bizet)
Crossroads Blues – Robert Johnson
Feel Like Going Home – Muddy Waters
I Was Made to Love Her – Stevie Wonder
Hard Times – Ray Charles
I Love the Woman – Freddie King
Purple Rain – Prince

Book: *Barnaby Rudge* (Charles Dickens)
Luxury: A guitar

PENELOPE LIVELY (September 17, 1989)

'Ruhe sanft, mein holdes Leben' from *Zaide* (Mozart)
Christmas Story (Schütz)
Howlin' at the Moon – George Jones
'Beim Schlafengehen' from *Four Last Songs* (R. Strauss)
Oboe Concerto (Haydn)
The Shepherd on the Rock (Schubert)
Nocturne in B flat minor Op. 9 No. 1 (Chopin)
Come Ye Sons of Art (Purcell)

Book: *Moby Dick* (Herman Melville)
Luxury: A pair of binoculars

JOHN OGDON (September 24, 1989)

'Dawn' from 'Four Sea Interludes' from *Peter Grimes* (Britten)
Piano Concerto No. 4 in G minor (Rachmaninov)
L'Ile joyeuse (Debussy)
Symphony No. 1 (Walton)
Piano Sonata in B minor (Liszt)
Tarantella from Suite No. 2 (Rachmaninov) – John Ogdon and Brenda Lucas
Piano Concerto No. 20 in D minor (Mozart)
La mer (Debussy) – Hallé Orchestra

Book: *The Moonstone* (Wilkie Collins)
Luxury: A Steinway grand piano

LUCINDA LAMBTON (October 1, 1989)

Impromptu in G flat Op. 90 No. 3 (Schubert)
Appenzeller (yodelling song)
Love Hurts – The Everly Brothers
A Four-legged Friend – Roy Rogers and Sons of the Pioneers
Quartet from *Fidelio* (Beethoven)
A Fool Such As I – Elvis Presley
Lost Lover Blues – Lottie Kimbrough
La Marseillaise

Book: *The Dictionary of National Biography*
Luxury: A word processor

JACK LEMMON (October 8, 1989)

Just One of Those Things – Art Tatum
Someone to Watch Over Me – George Gershwin
Goose Pimples – Bix Beiderbecke and His Gang
When the Saints Go Marching In
Piano Concerto No. 2 in C minor (Rachmaninov)
The World Is Waiting for the Sunrise – Benny Goodman Sextet
Double Violin Concerto (Bach)
Rhapsody in Blue (Gershwin)

Book: *A Play in the Fields of Our Lord* (Peter Matheson)
Luxury: A piano

ALAN PLATER (October 15, 1989)

Just A-sittin' and A-rockin' – Duke Ellington and Blanton-Webster Band
Do Not Go Gentle into that Good Night (Dylan Thomas) – read by the author
Lorelei – Ella Fitzgerald
When It's Ours – Alex Glasgow and John Woodvine
Misterioso – Thelonius Monk
Cryin' All Day – Frank Ricotti All Stars
Here (Philip Larkin) – read by the author
Fine and Mellow – Billie Holiday and Lester Young

Book: *Smell of Sunday Dinner* (Sid Chaplin)
Luxury: Writing materials

COLIN THUBRON (October 22, 1989)

'O tu che in seno agli angeli' from *The Force of Destiny* (Verdi) – Giovanni Martinelli
   (recorded in 1927)
Ceremony of Mevelvi whirling dervishes
Piano Concerto No. 23 in A (Mozart)
'Der Abschied' from *Das Lied von der Erde* (Mahler)
'Ich bin der Welt abhanden gekommen' from 'Rückert Songs' (Mahler) – Dame Janet
   Baker
String Quartet No. 14 in C sharp minor (Beethoven) – Lindsay String Quartet
'Die Nebensonnen' from *Die Winterreise* (Schubert)
Love Duet from Part 3 of *The Creation* (Haydn)

Book: *A Year of Grace* (Victor Gollancz)
Luxury: Scuba-diving equipment

IAN BOTHAM (November 5, 1989)

Get Off of My Cloud – The Rolling Stones
Symphony No. 3, 'Eroica' (Beethoven)
No Woman, No Cry – Bob Marley and the Wailers
Layla – Eric Clapton
1812 Overture (Tchaikovsky)
Yesterday – The Beatles
I'm Still Standing – Elton John
Pomp and Circumstance March No. 1 (Elgar)

Book: An encyclopaedia of species of fish of the world
Luxury: A fishing rod

MICHAEL CODRON (November 12, 1989)

Amapola – Julio Iglesias
Symphony in C (Bizet)
Pick Yourself Up – Fred Astaire and Ginger Rogers (tap dancing)
Concerto for Mandolin, Strings and Continuo (Vivaldi)
The Man I Love (Gershwin) – arranged and played by Percy Grainger
A Kind of Magic – Queen
Sing a Song With Me – Barbara Cook
When You Smile – Roberta Flack

Book: *Caroline and Charlotte* (Alison Plowman)
Luxury: A trunkload of jigsaw puzzles

SEAMUS HEANEY (November 19, 1989)

String Quartet No. 13 in B flat (Beethoven)
An buinnean bui (The yellow bittern) – Joe Heaney
My Aunt Jane (Belfast street song)
O Lord Give Thy Holy Spirit (Tallis)
Extract from *Malone Dies* (Samuel Beckett) – Jack MacGowran
Nocturne No. 1 in E flat (John Field)
Piano Quintet in A, 'Trout' (Schubert)
Believe Me if all those Endearing Young Charms – John McCormack

Book: *Ulysses* (James Joyce)
Luxury: A pair of 'Doc Martens'' boots

LADY MOSLEY (November 26, 1989)

Symphony No. 41 (Mozart)
'Casta diva' from *Norma* (Bellini)
'Ode to Joy' from Symphony No. 9, 'Choral' (Beethoven)
Love Duet from Act 1 of *Die Walküre* (Wagner) – Maria Müller and Wolfgang Windgassen
'Liebestod' from *Tristan and Isolde* (Wagner)
'Habañera' from *Carmen* (Bizet)
A Whiter Shade of Pale – Procol Harum
Polonaise in F sharp minor Op. 44 (Chopin)

Book: *Remembrance of Things Past* (Marcel Proust)
Luxury: A soft pillow or rug

NIGEL LAWSON (December 3, 1989)

Clarinet Quintet in A Major (Mozart)
Jesu, Joy of Man's Desiring (Bach) – Dame Myra Hess (the castaway's great-aunt)
Don't Make Fun of the Fair – Noël Coward
Act 3 of *Der Rosenkavalier* (R. Strauss)
'Nimrod' from the *Enigma Variations* (Elgar)
Piano Quintet in A, 'Trout' (Schubert)
Yada Yada – Dory Previn
Variations on 'God save the King' (Beethoven)

Book: The poetry of John Donne
Luxury: A solar-powered radio set

PAULINE COLLINS (December 17, 1989)

I'll Remember April – Erroll Garner
Toccata from Organ Symphony No. 5 (Widor)
Got My Mojo Working – Jimmy Smith
La gitane et l'oiseau – Mado Robin
And I'm Telling You I'm Not Going – Jennifer Holliday
Violin Concerto (Tchaikovsky)
Clair de lune (Debussy)
'Amor ti vieta' from *Fedora* (Giordano)

Book: A teach-yourself book about physics
Luxury: Paper and pencils

HRH THE DUCHESS OF KENT (December 24, 1989)

Piano Sonata in D, K284 (Mozart)
Symphony No. 6, 'Pathétique' (Tchaikovsky)
Tuba Tune (Norman Cocker) – Francis Jackson (organ of York Minster)
Double Violin Concerto (Bach)
'Che gelida manina' from *La Bohème* (Puccini)
Cello Concerto (Elgar) – Jacqueline du Pré
Maxwell's Silver Hammer – The Beatles
'Ave verum corpus' (Mozart)

Book: *Reader's Digest New Do-It-Yourself Manual*
Luxury: A solar-powered lamp

DIRK BOGARDE (December 31, 1989)

The end of Act 2 of *Tosca* (Puccini)
La fileuse (Raff) – Yvonne Arnaud
Symphony in D minor (Franck)
Je t'aime – Yvonne Printemps
Adagietto from Symphony No. 5 (Mahler)
Piano Concerto No. 1 (Liszt)
Waltz sequence from *Der Rosenkavalier* (R. Strauss)
New York, New York – Boston Pops Orchestra

Book: *Akenfield* (Ronald Blythe)
Luxury: A distillery

PS

Finally, with some reluctance, but at the insistence of my publisher, here are the records, book and luxury I chose when I appeared on the programme with Michael Parkinson:

Rhapsody on a Theme of Paganini (Rachmaninov)
Love Duet from *La Bohème* (Puccini)
Hey Jude – The Beatles
'Sound the Trumpet' from *Come Ye Sons of Art* (Purcell)
In the Bleak Mid-winter – King's College Choir, Cambridge
Four Seasons (T.S. Eliot) – Sir John Gielgud
Lady With the Braid – Dory Previn
Every Time We Say Goodbye – Ella Fitzgerald

Book: Elizabeth David's *French Provincial Cooking*
Luxury: Iron and ironing board